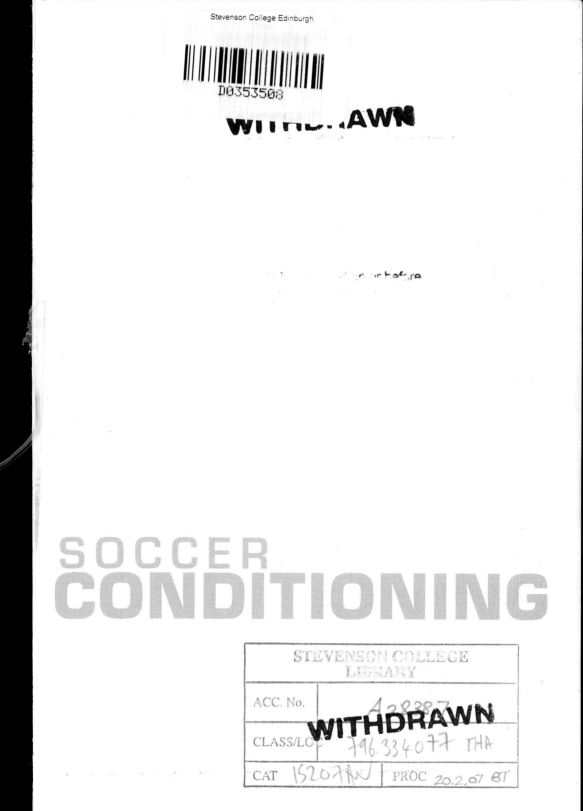
SOCCER CONDITIONING

'Having worked with Simon as both a player and a coach for many years, I have always found him to be fastidious in his preparation. Through his encouragement and empathy with players, he has always managed to get the best out of them in an aspect of professional football that most do not enjoy. His thirst for knowledge is insatiable, and whilst understanding the science, he always approaches coaching with a great deal of common sense.'

Tony Mowbray
Hibernian manager
Former Ipswich Town player/coach

'Simon's experience of working with elite athletes, combined with his common sense and ceaseless drive for learning, make this book invaluable for anyone interested in physical fitness.'

Willie Donachie
Millwall assistant manager
Former Ipswich Town assistant manager and Scotland international

'I have had the pleasure of working with Simon both on and off the field of play. He brings with him an extensive knowledge, as well as an infectious enthusiasm for fitness. Simon has the unique ability to address the needs of a team both individually and collectively. This has led to increased fitness levels and performance of the team as a whole, and has played a major role in our sustained success.'

Jason De Vos
Ipswich Town captain
Former Canada international

'I first met Simon when I joined Ipswich Town on loan. As I had just recovered from injury, I had one or two conditioning issues, which Simon solved promptly and in a professional and imaginative way. He made conditioning enjoyable, rather than a chore. He has always managed to put the science into practice in a most effective manner, and is one of the best fitness coaches that I have worked with.'

David Unsworth
Sheffield United defender
Former Ipswich Town player and England international

SOCCER
CONDITIONING

SIMON THADANI

A & C BLACK • LONDON

First published 2006 by A&C Black Publishers Ltd
38 Soho Square, London W1D 3HB
www.acblack.com

ISBN-10 0 7136 7673 6
ISBN-13 978 0 7136 7673 0

A CIP catalogue record for this book is available from the British Library.

Typeset in Celeste by Palimpsest Book Production Ltd, Grangemouth, Stirlingshire

Note: It is always the responsibility of the individual to assess his or her own fitness capability before participating in any training activity. While every effort has been made to ensure
the content of this book is as technically accurate as possible, neither the author nor the
publishers can accept responsibility for any injury or loss sustained as a result of the use of
this material.

Cover image © Action Images
Illustrations © Mark Silver

A&C Black uses paper produced with elemental chlorine-free pulp, harvested from managed
sustainable forests.

Printed and bound in Great Britain by MPG Books Ltd, Bodmin

CONTENTS

ACKNOWLEDGEMENTS

I wish to thank Ipswich Town Football Club for giving me the opportunity to work in the professional game of football. In the eight years I have been involved in conditioning at Ipswich Town with the first team I have witnessed the highs of their promotion to Premiership football and European football (two successive seasons in the UEFA Cup). I have also witnessed the club's lows: relegation to the Championship – a league with more teams and fixtures, and a play-off system that further extends the domestic season and makes conditioning even more critical – administration and play-off disappointments. I have also worked for three different managers and several coaches. All this has taught me a great deal, including how circumstances out of your control affect the world of conditioning and how you must adapt while sticking to your principles.

I would not have gained insight into the game and been able to write this book without the assistance, vision and forward thinking of David Sheepshanks (Ipswich chairman) and George Burley (manager until 2002); the experience, common sense and perception of Joe Royle (manager until 2006) and Willie Donachie (coach until 2006); and the knowledge, professionalism and open minds of coaches Tony Mowbray, Bryan Klug and the late Dale Roberts. I wish to pass on my deepest thanks to them for making me a better conditioning coach.

I also wish to thank Dave Williams (physio), Matt Byard (physio) and Frank Dick (consultant) for their specialist assistance. It is, and has to be, a partnership.

I also wish to show my appreciation to my partner Nicky and children Zac, Amy and Max for being my inspiration in writing this book.

Finally, I wish to thank Robert Foss at A&C Black Publishers for teaching me and guiding me while writing this book. Without his help, it would still be an idea, not an end product.

FOREWORD

Anyone who knows anything about the game of soccer is aware of just how much the game has progressed in terms of training and fitness over the last few years. In the past, players were expected to turn up for regular training but were trusted to keep themselves fit and healthy. And in days gone by, the post-match refreshment was likely to be a pint of beer not an isotonic drink!

Now, thanks to fitness professionals like Simon Thadani, players are staying fitter and better conditioned than ever throughout their careers. When I joined Ipswich from Sheffield Wednesday in 1999, Simon had already been working wonders for a number of years at the club. Our success in getting promotion to the Premiership in the 1999/2000 season, and finishing fifth in the top league in the world the following year, was in no small part down to Simon's professional approach to all aspects of fitness and his conditioning programmes at Ipswich Town. Simon's advice and techniques enabled me to continue at a high level right to the end of my playing career, aged 37. It is also no coincidence that a number of 'home-grown' academy graduates have gone on to be top-class players both at Ipswich and elsewhere, playing at Premiership level and for their respective countries.

Soccer Conditioning is a unique and indispensable book for soccer coaches at every level of the game, from amateur Sunday-league to Premier League. It not only details the development of every important physical aspect of conditioning, but also the mental toughness needed to stay one step ahead in today's game. Simon's tried and tested methods have developed from his own awareness of different situations and changing players' needs, and a learning curve over many years, with plenty of 'trial and error'!

I look forward to working with Simon for many more years as we take Ipswich Town into a new era.

Jim Magilton
Ipswich Town manager
July 2006

INTRODUCTION

The aim of this book is to give fitness conditioners, soccer coaches, teachers, or indeed any football enthusiast, a new and fresh perspective on conditioning players. Whatever the age and level of the players you work with, this book will be relevant to you. It is based on my own successes and failures in the professional and amateur game, working with adults and children.

I have been fortunate enough to be instructing and teaching for nearly 17 years, during which time I was lucky enough to get involved with Ipswich Town Football Club back in the early nineties – I'm still there now – first as a qualified soccer coach and then as a conditioner. From the outset, I was surprised to see how conditioning was applied to adults and children, and the same questions kept coming to mind:

- Is the conditioning specific to the game?
- What are the demands of the game?
- What standards do you need to achieve?
- Is the level of fitness required specific to a player's position?
- What drills or sessions can help achieve these aims?

More often than not, it seemed that current drills and sessions had just been passed on from one generation of coaches to the next without anybody ever looking into the benefits. I was creating more questions than answers!

I decided to start from scratch – I read as many books as I could, collected articles, attended courses and workshops, and watched videos. More importantly, I decided to talk to as many people as I could – players, coaches, managers, sports scientists – to help me create a picture of the perfectly conditioned player, with fitness achievements that were specific to his position. I had started to answer some of my questions.

Some ten years later – I now have eight years' experience with adults and eleven years' with children – I believe I have many of the answers. During this time, I have seen conditioning change significantly throughout soccer. For me, gone are the days when players used to run six or seven miles on roads, train hard the day after the match, do speed work in long sand pits, run up and down stadium terraces or do weight training just for the sake of it. Although I am not saying that this is entirely the wrong approach (indeed there may have been some very noticeable benefits), conditioning has become more updated, relevant and fresh. Conditioning is now at the forefront of soccer, and scientific research allows us to understand the demands of the game much better.

Soccer is not a science, but science can improve players' conditioning, having a positive impact on their physical performance on the pitch, which will in turn assist their technical performance. As a very important component of a player's overall make-up in the modern game, conditioning should be as much about the player himself – his honesty, belief in his ability and desire to achieve – as proper coaching with the application of common sense in the right environment.

Every team and individual wants to be stronger, fitter and quicker than the opposition. To achieve this, you either have to be more naturally gifted or better conditioned than your opponents – and to achieve the latter you must do something that gives your players the edge. That is what *Soccer Conditioning* is all about – new ideas, methods and ways of thinking.

Scientific advances, showing more accurately than ever the demands of the game through improved testing and monitoring tools, can be combined with better education to make conditioning more relevant than ever before. Putting science into practice (regardless of the age and level at which you are working) is not easy; in fact, it is often the stumbling block over which I have seen many good professional and amateur conditioning coaches trip and fall (sometimes losing their job in the process). In this book, I hope to show you how the science can be put into practice in simple, easy and varied ways. If you can improve one player, he becomes fitter, which in turn improves not only him, but also the team. In most amateur soccer this becomes even more relevant, because the standards differ so much. The fitter you are, the more this will help your technical side. With children, this approach allows you to lay the foundation for later years, giving them the advantage of a head start.

For me, the secret of conditioning in soccer is to put the theory into good practice. It must be specific to soccer and relevant to the age, position and individual circumstances of the players that you are working with. It must be varied, fresh and enjoyable (especially when working with younger players). If you ensure that players are aware of the benefits, they will willingly participate.

It is essential that you have a goal to aim for. I once read that the ultimate goal in soccer should be 'the ability to compete in a game of soccer for its entire duration with the minimum depreciation in skill level due to fatigue.' Although I do not disagree with this, after working in both the amateur and professional game for many years I have adapted this to be more realistic – 'the ability to complete a game of soccer with the fitness and conditioning aspect being a positive component for its entire duration, regardless of a win, draw or loss'. If you can achieve this, you will have done extremely well.

On many occasions, I have heard people blame lack of fitness if the team is on a losing run or if the manager is under pressure. Don't let conditioning be a cheap excuse for a bad performance; it is a component that cannot easily be quantified.

The structure of the book

I have attempted to outline a step-by-step approach in this book – read from start to finish it will guide you through all the key aspects and avoid the pitfalls of soccer conditioning as I see them. However, depending on your experience and goals – or whether you have read the book all the way through already – you can easily dip in and out of the book for specific guidance. For such readers, here is a brief overview of the chapters.

Chapter 1 sets out my beliefs on soccer conditioning, the standards that I have adopted over the years as I developed a more thorough insight into my trade and the demands of the game. I look at the tools we have available to us in the professional game to analyse conditioning – and the lessons that can be learned from these for all levels of the sport – and how I have adapted my conditioning sessions and principles accordingly. I will also take a brief look at the basic theory of training.

In **Chapter 2** I will discuss planning and its importance over a season. I will also look at pre-season and the importance of friendlies – this can be the foundation of the season and can get players (professionals, amateurs and children alike) noticed. Every manager and coach loves running power! It will show you a two-week schedule to help build up strength and stamina. This chapter will also talk about the close season and how this influences pre-season.

Chapter 3 is specific to the conditioning of young players – they are not, as is often believed in soccer, 'mini adults'. They have very specific physiological needs which depend on many factors, only one of which is their age. This chapter explains these differences and highlights the specifics that you need to be aware of. It also sets new standards for conditioning children.

Chapter 4 is about speed – *the* competitive edge. For me, when all other components are just about equal, players with pace will always win out. I look at both mental and physical aspects, discuss the 'dos and don'ts', and again set benchmarks to aim for.

In **Chapter 5** I look at the importance of testing and how it is essential to be clear *why* you are testing and *what* you are testing before you start the stopwatch and send players off round the pitch. For me, the benefit of testing comes in recording a player's progress and monitoring their performance against their own standards. However, I have also included in this chapter a number of benchmark results which can be used for comparison.

For many readers, **Chapter 6** will be the well thumbed part of the book. It covers my favourite 50 tried and tested conditioning drills that I have used with adults and children. In my experience, there is no substitute for drills which have specific and measurable outcomes: they give you an objective measure. The sessions I will show you are mainly aerobic and anaerobic, speed drills (with and without the ball) and some power drills. I will also show you some basic drills for the gymnasium and swimming pool.

During my time in the game, I have had handed down – and have learned the hard way – many tips on conditioning. **Chapter 7** brings these together and they will hopefully serve you as well as they do me. The majority of these lessons have been learned at the highest levels of the game, but like all true wisdom they apply to every level – from Europe to the Sunday-league pitch.

Throughout the book I have also scattered some 'briefs' and 'myths'. The principles of soccer conditioning will improve the performance of your players and your team, but only if you address a number of other issues – rest, recovery, dehydration, diet and nutrition, etc. Each of these topics is another book in its own right, so in the 'briefs' I have attempted to highlight the key points and to steer you in the right direction for more information. The 'myths' are just that – old wives' tales that have grown up around soccer conditioning. It is time that they were put to rest once and for all.

I hope this book will assist you in conditioning your players, and give you the practical tips and ideas you need to allow your players to reach their full potential. Here's hoping that your team has plenty of running left in their legs come the end of the season for that unexpected cup final!

One last thing: throughout the book I have referred to players as 'he'. This is due to the fact that most of my career has been spent coaching men's and boys' teams, and also to avoid the unsightly 'he/she', 'him/her' combinations. All my advice and guidance applies equally to male and female teams and players, so please read 'she' for 'he', etc.

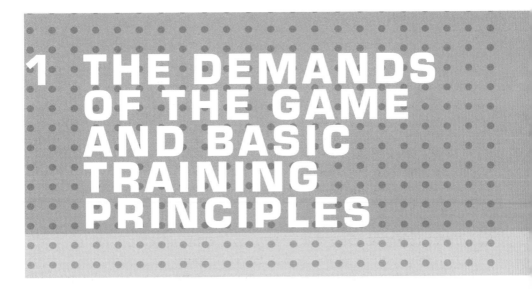

1 THE DEMANDS OF THE GAME AND BASIC TRAINING PRINCIPLES

Before you plan a conditioning programme, you must understand the physical demands of the game. This will have a direct impact on which drills to use, their frequency and intensity, and the time spent on them.

This chapter will cover the following:
- The demands of the game – positions and formations and how these affect the team and individuals.
- The basic training principles – the key components.

What is Prozone?

Throughout this book, I make extensive use of statistics to emphasise a point and suggest certain approaches to conditioning. These statistics are based on four years' data collected at Portman Road using the Prozone system, so it is worth giving you a quick overview of what it is all about.

Since the introduction of Prozone, approximately 25 games have been covered in a typical season – mainly home games, and either league fixtures (Premiership and Football League Championship) or cup ties (UEFA Cup, FA Cup and League Cup).

Prozone is an independent company which provides clubs with a hi-tech system that gives unbelievably detailed analysis of players' performances for every home match and some away games. It consists of a tracking software system, using nine cameras situated strategically around the stadium, which cross-section every part of the pitch. All 22 players are always in view – there is nowhere to hide! Prozone monitors every pass, tackle and header, as well as movement on and off the ball.

In terms of fitness and conditioning, it measures:

- Total distance covered.
- High intensity runs.
- Speed.
- Movement profile (intensity).
- Number of runs at sprint and high intensity.
- Top speeds (as well as acceleration/deceleration).
- All of the above, both with and without the ball.

TRAINING MYTH

'If I stop training my muscle will turn to fat.'

Muscle and fat are different types of human tissue, therefore one cannot turn into the other when you stop training. You will lose muscle mass as you are not overloading the muscles.

The list is seemingly endless. The information from the game is downloaded, sent to Prozone head office, processed and returned in 24–30 hours.

For me, the comprehensive physical analysis of both teams that Prozone produces is the best way of testing a player's physical state (subject to variables, see box on page 3). If a player cannot perform to their physical maximum in front of 25,000 supporters, then when can they?

AMATEUR SOCCER PLAYERS

From talking to many conditioning and soccer coaches in the amateur game and working with amateur players (including some basic testing, depending on variation in the standard of both professional and amateur players) there is approximately a 10–20% difference between the professional and amateur game in physical condition of players.

All the statistics I use in this book are based on Football League Championship players, so if you intend to use them as benchmarks for your amateur players, you will have to make reductions depending on the level at which the team plays and how fit you want your players to be.

The Demands of the Game

Prozone has given me a fresh insight into the physical demands of the game and I have adapted my drills, sessions and principles accordingly. These statistics will also be of benefit to you – they will give you a greater understanding of the demands of the game for specific positions and should help you design your drills and the FITT (Frequency, Intensity, Type and Time) sessions for your players, which will be relevant to their positions.

BEWARE VARIABLES!

When using Prozone, you must be aware that there are variables which may distort the analysis of the team and individual. Many of the variables can become manageable when compared with past history data and examples/standards, and by talking to the coaches about tactics. These variables are just as relevant to the amateur game as to the professional, if not more so. Variables which can affect physical performance include:

1. Individual players – do not compare a 21-year-old to a 36-year-old. Do not compare a holding midfielder to an attacking midfielder, etc.

2. Mentality/attitude – at both individual and team level, e.g. lifestyle problems (individual) or playing for a winning or losing team (team).

3. Tactics – your own and the opposition's, e.g. there will be obvious differences if you compare an attack-minded team with a defensive side.

4. Time of season – see the graphs on pages 7–8, which show the possible effects of the time of year.

5. Match situation – chasing the game for a win or happy for a draw.

6. Time of kick-off (3pm or 8pm); interestingly, this appears to affect physical performance.

7. Pitch and weather conditions – hot days to soft pitches.

8. Previous schedule – two games in three days, four games in nine days, etc.

9. Finally, it is interesting to note that generally the team that has less possession in a game tends to do more running than the team with more possession.

Analysing position-specific performance

The following statistics are based on performance over a season in the Championship. They cover 26 matches – 23 at home and three away.

KEY

DC = Distance Covered
HI = High Intensity distance covered (5.5m/s – 7.0m/s)
SD = Sprint Distance Covered (7.0m/s+)
m/s = metres per second

3-5-2 FORMATION

	DC 11.07km	DC 11.04km	DC 10.90km	
	HI 563m	HI 513m	HI 501m	
	SD 104m	SD 96m	SD 89m	

DC 11.32km	DC 12.22km	DC 12.76km	DC 12.95km	DC 12.06km
HI 805m	HI 870m	HI 905m	HI 1240m	HI 1040m
SD 175m	SD 143m	SD 125m	SD 260m	SD 259m

	DC 10.20km	DC 11.90km	
	HI 905m	HI 1195m	
	SD 252m	SD 334m	

4-4-2 FORMATION

DC 10.88km	DC 10.48km	DC 10.22km	DC 11.20km
HI 787m	HI 715m	HI 710m	HI 1170m
SD 160m	SD 150m	SD 179m	SD 325m

DC 12.55km	DC 12.34km	DC 12.23km	DC 12.45km
HI 1143m	HI 1175m	HI 828m	HI 1450m
SD 210m	SD 225m	SD 132m	SD 342m

	DC 9.74km	DC 11.57km	
	HI 870m	HI 1272m	
	SD 258m	SD 366m	

These player averages show the 'position-specific' individual requirements and physical effort that is needed throughout a season, using a 3–5–2 formation, or a 4–4–2 formation.

The figures are very interesting and allow you to differentiate between the physical demands placed on players according to their position and the formation that the team plays. Using the data above, a few things are immediately apparent:

- **Centre backs** (who tend to cover the least distance in high-intensity work than any other position) – there is a definite difference in the physical requirements of the 4–4–2 formation and the 3–5–2 formation.

- **Full backs** – they cover much more ground when used in the wing back role of the 3–5–2 formation, when compared to less dynamic 4–4–2 system.
- **Midfielders** (tend to cover the most distance in whatever formation) – they do less speed work in a 3–5–2 formation, and more high intensity work in a 4–4–2 formation.
- **Strikers** – cover less distance than most of the other outfield players (except centre backs), but do more work in the sprint distance zone.

Again, it is worth pointing out that the above is subject to the individuality and desire of the players and the managers, and the tactics being employed. For example, the manager may tell his full backs not to do any offence work, or tell one or two midfielders to do a holding job. However, it is invaluable in that it sets standards and benchmarks for players as individuals, subject to their position, and helps to identify the physical position-specific demands of the game.

This can be very useful if you are not sure of a player's position, especially with amateurs and children. For example, you may have a young player who is very skilful and quick; your instinct may be to play him in an attacking midfield role, using his pace and tricks to provide that 'killer' ball. But he has a weakness – he takes a long time to recover from each sprint. Take a look at the benchmarks above and it quickly becomes clear that his most suited position may well be as a striker. Try him for a few games and see how he goes. This is the key to using this data – use it to guide your training and player management, not as a set of commandments that players have to follow with no allowance.

TRAINING BRIEF – NUTRITION

Nutritional advice in football has made considerable progress over the last 15 years and plays an important role in performance. Food is the body's fuel, and the better quality fuel you put in the better the performance you will get from the body, day in, day out.

Nowadays, professional players are very well educated about nutrition (they often learn about nutrition in their Academy education). It is basically common sense. Remember, the food consumed not only gives energy but it also assists growth and repair (of injuries) and maintains general body function.

My simple nutritional tips:
* Understand the basic importance of carbohydrates, proteins and fat, and their required levels.
* Ensure your energy (food) intake approximately equals your energy output (for the normal player).

* Never miss breakfast. It is a very important meal.

* There is no harm in having treats but keep them in moderation.

* Do not abuse your body because it will eventually catch up with you.

* No single food contains all the nutrients we need for health so try to eat a wide range of foods each day.

* Eat at least five portions of fruit and vegetables a day.

* Starchy foods such as bread, pasta, rice, potatoes and cereals should be the main part of meals and snacks.

* Meat and fish are good sources of protein, vitamins and minerals.

* Milk is also a good source of protein, vitamins and minerals; it is an excellent source of calcium, which is particularly important for bones, especially during growth.

* Eat small portions and regularly, not one or two big meals a day. Not eating for long periods is not beneficial.

* Snacks are important, especially before and after exercise, i.e. fruit/dried fruit, cereal, yoghurt, toast, energy bars, low fat biscuits, etc.

Nutrition is not my speciality so it is one of the areas where I always seek help from a nutritionist for detailed advice, and I suggest you do the same. There are also plenty of good books available on the subject.

Analysing team performance

These following figures are for three full seasons (each of nine months):

* 02/03 season, club finished 7th in the Football League Championship.
* 03/04 season, club finished 5th in the Football League Championship.
* 04/05 season, club finished 3rd in the Football League Championship.

They are based on distance covered, high intensity covered and sprint distance covered, and cover all players (including the goalkeeper).

The first graph shows the average distance covered per player per game (it includes everything from walking to jogging, running and sprinting) at different stages of the season. Remember that distance covered is basically aerobic endurance. Statistics can be interpreted in many ways; the graphs show how we have interpreted them. It is interesting to see how the team, in all three seasons, gradually improves as the season progresses and how it plateaus about the time of the Christmas cycle, mainly due to the number of games and the inability to implement player rotation due to there being small squads during these periods.

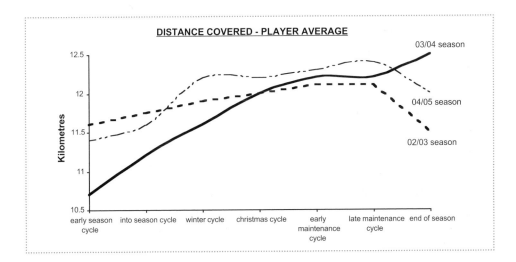

What concerns me is how the team's performance dips at the end of the season for two out of the three seasons in this graph. I cannot give a definite reason for this because I have not got enough data (variables). It is also interesting to note that in our best season, 04/05 (we finished third in the league and had our best conditioning results to date), all three graph lines dip on the last cycle. Is it because of the pressure of automatic promotion and play-offs, or is it because the players were tired; or did they perform above expectations and then just burn out? Or was it something else?

High intensity work is measured in metres and is anything over 5.5 metres per second. The curves are similar to the distance covered graph but perhaps a little

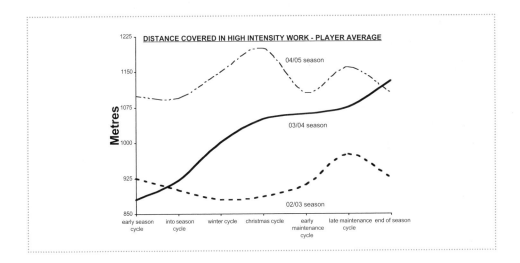

more erratic. When the media describes a game as 'high energy' or 'high tempo', it usually means high intensity. Many of the same conclusions from the previous graph are appropriate for this graph, except that the graph line for the 04/05 season (our best) is more erratic due to high intensity. Also, sprint work is down to individual ability – some are natural sprinters, some not, it is 'nature not nurture' – and losing top players with pace to injury or suspension and replacing them with 'lesser' players will naturally affect and distort team statistics. If players are tired, speed and power tend to be the first to suffer. These conclusions are also appropriate to the graph below.

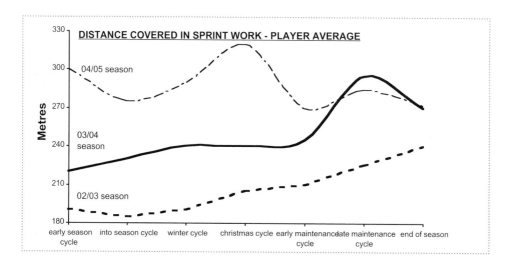

Sprint work is defined as anything over 7.0 metres per second. I believe sprint work can be the difference in winning or losing – the edge. (See Chapter 4.) The graph curve lines tend to be shallower, especially in the first few months of the season, and then become more erratic, but basically follow the same pattern. Like high intensity work, speed is one of the areas we have been trying to develop as a club over the last few years.

Finally, the upturn shown after the Christmas cycle (shown in eight of the nine graph lines) can be interpreted in several ways, but for me it proves that good planning, monitoring the players' physical condition, and toning down and variation, all have a positive impact on training. It's a marathon and not a sprint.

The above graphs are just a few examples of how we look at team conditioning performance throughout the season.

Once the variables have been eliminated and managed (e.g. the effect of the extremely hot weather at the start of the 03/04 season), we can begin to monitor aspects and ask questions such as:

- Are the players in peak condition at the beginning of, and during, the season?
- When do they reach their peak?
- Does conditioning dip, and if so, why?
- Does burnout and fatigue become a factor for the team?
- Is there a relationship between the team's physical performance and injuries?

Above all else, the three main aspects of monitoring that you need to consider are:
- How does the team compare to last season?
- How does the team compare to the opposition?
- How does the physical training during the week affect the players on match days?

By monitoring all of the above, and talking to the manager, coaches and players, you will learn many lessons about training, conditioning and the preparation of individuals for the actual games.

Note that the training, conditioning and preparation for our actual group of players may not work for other groups, and that certain individuals are treated differently according to their own requirements.

'Every player is unique. Don't worry about what other players do, concentrate on your-self when it comes to conditioning. Ensure that you work to your own maximum ability.'
Jim Magilton, Ipswich Town manager, former Northern Ireland captain, over 700 Premiership and League appearances

Analysing individual performance

The individual players' graphs that show their performance throughout the season are very similar to the team performance graphs in respect to trends, with two main differences:
- The graph plot is more erratic. This is mainly due to the manager's tactics, the opposition team's tactics and formation, and the individual opposition players in terms of varying pace and skill. A player's form is far more variable than the team as a whole.
- If a player is out of the team (injured or not selected) for several games, the more explosive components (such as speed) tend to suffer more than the aerobic components (such as distance covered). This is commonly known as match fitness. This is why players coming back from injury tend to be substituted during the second half or start on the subs' bench. See page 16 for some of our

findings. Reserve team games are also a way of compensating a player for being out for several weeks, as long as he has the right attitude!

Performance data for comparison

The tables beginning on page 11 give you an idea of how we can use the data from Prozone to compare the physical state of individuals and the team, both against each other and the opposition. They are also useful for you as a coach and trainer as they give you benchmark figures to monitor the performance of your players. Of course, it's a bit unfair to expect a Sunday-league full back to cover the same sort of distance or achieve the same top speed as a Premier League player but it is not too much to ask that his sprints, runs, jogs and time spent walking are of a similar ratio to the top players.

Whether you are a professional, amateur or youth footballer, the statistics can give you an idea of the demands of the game at the top level. Remember that an amateur player is approximately 10–20% less fit than a professional, depending on the standard of football they are playing.

A typical example of a match overview/physical summary of a team's performance (including goalkeepers)

Prozone is great for comparing the physical performance of the team with that of the opposition. When combined with the possession-of-the-ball statistics it can give some very interesting results, which may not otherwise be obvious from the match score. In this particular example, Ipswich (the home team) comfortably won the game, which was virtually over as a contest after 60 minutes (3–0 up), perhaps accounting for the poor performance of the away team and the below-average team statistics (see table below). When analysing the first 30 minutes of the game, the statistics were good for the home team and below average for the away team due to the fact that they came to defend (roughly a 4–5–1 formation) and only threaten Ipswich on the break. This game was certainly not a high tempo game. Does the home team cover more ground than the away team? This is a very interesting question, which my analysis shows depends on tactics, the state of the game, the mentality of the crowd and, of course, fitness. In my experience, these statistics are always very popular with the executives and board members of a club – they like to know the players are putting the effort in for their wages!

'Hard work, dedication and a positive attitude are the keys to success in conditioning. Show your character, not only when things are going well but also when you receive a setback.'

Jason De Vos, Ipswich captain

Home Team	Physical	Away Team
120.6km	Overall Distance Covered	116.7km
2.4km	Distance Covered – sprints	2.2km
7.9km	Distance Covered – HS runs	7.0km
1281	No. of High Int. Activities	1117
9.4m/s	Top Speed	9.4m/s
46secs	Average recovery time	53secs

A typical example of individual movement breakdown – 90 minutes completed (distances in km)

The movement breakdown table is a very good tool when designing your conditioning drills. It measures the intensity levels during the game, which can then be transferred to specific drills to assist progression and overload. An example of this would be sprint drills, covering 21m+ in three seconds (after the initial acceleration phase), with a recovery time specific to the player's position. The table also shows how much time players spent walking, which is useful in helping to design a drill with active recovery (walking).

	Walk Below 2.5m/s (km)	Jog 2.5m/s–4.0m/s (km)	Run 4.0 m/s–5.5m/s (km)	HSR 5.5m/s–7.0m/s (km)	Sprint 7.0m/s+ (km)
Goalkeeper	3.73	1.48	0.28	0.05	0.00(1)
Right Back	3.70	4.33	1.65	0.57	0.15(21)
Centre Back	3.74	4.46	1.71	0.65	0.20(28)
Centre Back	3.93	4.11	1.46	0.41	0.12(21)
Left Back	3.52	4.51	1.73	0.78	0.30(38)
Central Midfield	3.17	5.54	2.73	0.92	0.20(28)
Central Midfield	3.20	5.65	2.70	1.21	0.30(47)
Left Midfield	3.51	5.33	2.38	0.81	0.14(26)
Centre Forward	4.07	4.15	1.47	0.85	0.66(65)
Centre Forward	3.78	4.60	1.95	1.00	0.40(45)

Brackets – number of sprints.

A typical example of mean time between high intensity activity (high intensity activity is any activity above 5.5 m/s)

Full back 62secs	Right midfielder 44secs	Centre forward 46secs
Centre back 49secs	Central midfielder 38secs	Centre forward 39secs
Centre back 85secs	Central midfielder 26secs	Sub 29secs
Full back 37secs	Left midfielder 42secs	

The position-specific mean time between high intensity activities is another great tool to help you design a conditioning drill, with or without a ball. For example, a central midfielder is working in the high intensity zone every 26 or 38 seconds. The time he spends in this zone can vary from a few seconds to up to 40 seconds. To support this workload you may want to introduce a simple interval training session for the midfielder, e.g. playing head tennis for 26–38 seconds and then doing a maximum of three penalty box to penalty box runs in 40 seconds.

It is all about matching the drills to the real life experience of the player on the pitch – you're unlikely to have the luxury of Prozone, but some careful observation of your players during a match (be sure to write your thoughts down at the time, in case you forget) will soon pay off if you then develop conditioning drills to match the style of play.

Example of time (seconds/minutes) spent in sprints, high-speed runs and runs during a match

Finally, the time period table gives you an idea of how much time is spent in the different intensity zones throughout a game. The zones are:

	Sprints (7.0m/s+)	High-speed runs (5.5–7.0m/s)	Runs (4.0–5.5m/s)
Goalkeeper	1.5secs	16secs	1.13mins
Full Back	56secs	2.45mins	7.07mins
Centre Back	23.5secs	1.50mins	6.49mins
Wide Midfield	16secs	1.29mins	5.24mins
Central Midfield	20secs	2.00mins	9.26mins
Centre Forward	63secs	2.40mins	7.39mins

It is interesting to note that the top performers of each team spent approximately 38 minutes of a 90-minute game moving at 2.5m/s (jogging) and above, turning a couple of hundred times plus, and changing direction several hundred times during this 38-minute period. This is invaluable information for designing drills, especially length of time.

THE REASONS BEHIND IMPROVEMENT AT IPSWICH

As you will have noticed from the earlier graphs, there has been good year-on-year improvement in the fitness of Ipswich players. Much of the credit for this must go to the players themselves for having the right attitude, and the manager and coaches bringing physically better players into the club.

But there are other factors, including:
- Players' desire, passion, and work ethic.
- Lessons learned from previous seasons.
- Better training methods (intensity).
- Better planning.
- Improved implementation of recovery methods.
- Players' natural physical progression.
- Higher general standards.

Fatigue

No matter how well conditioned players are, they will suffer from some element of fatigue during the course of a match. It is impossible to avoid, but it is possible to minimise the impact this has on performance.

The table on page 14 (taken over five Championship games – home and away matches) shows the extent to which fatigue was an issue by comparing performance in the first 15 minutes and the last 15 minutes

TRAINING MYTH

'If I wear more clothes and sweat more I will lose weight.'

We sweat to disperse the heat generated when exercising, so wearing more clothes can be dangerous. Also you may lose weight temporarily due to sweating but the liquids must be replaced or you will lose stamina and power, and feel dehydrated.

of a match. This is invaluable in helping to assess levels of fatigue (although, as with all comparisons, allowances have to be made for variables, such as the game situation, tactics and mentality). Statistics are for the team (ten outfield players). Substitutes are included, with an average of just below two substitutions per team, per game.

	First 15 minutes of game	Last 15 minutes of game
Total distance covered by the team	20. 9km	22.1km
High intensity distance covered by the team	1.5km	1.4km
Sprint work distance covered by the team	0.52km	0.54km
High intensity activities by the team	272 activities	260 activities

As you can see, the fatigue levels are surprisingly less than might have been expected in the professional game (but it does include the substitutes) although I expect the amateurs (subject to standard) and children to be much more. Even with the subs taken out of the equation, leaving eight outfield players on average, the difference is still less than expected!

A look at Premiership players

There has been much debate over the years about whether Premiership players are fitter than Championship players. Many conditioners say that Premiership players are fitter; however, according to my analysis (comparing 4–4–2 formations) Championship players definitely cover greater distances and do more high intensity work in a game, with distances covered in sprint work being similar. See page 4 for Championship stats and table on page 16 covering Premiership players. The big difference I have noticed between the two leagues in my analysis over the years is that Premiership players do, in general, beat Championship players when it comes to top speeds and explosive work, e.g. you would see five to seven Premiership players regularly hitting top speeds of 9.2m/s+, whereas in the Championship you would expect four or five maximum. This may show that Championship players work harder, but the real quality, the edge (see Chapter 4), is with Premiership players. This may also be relevant to all standards of amateur and children's leagues.

TRAINING BRIEF – HYDRATION

Much research has been done recently on dehydration. Figures such as '2% loss in body weight can lead to a greater than 30% fall in performance' or '3% loss in hydration in weight can decrease strength by 10% and speed by 8%', have been revealed. In our experience, players' weight pre- to post-match varied. We found some players had lost 2–3kg in body weight after 90 minutes, with the average being about 1–1.25kg. This is despite these players insisting they drank at half-time and during the game, which makes me wonder what happens in the amateur game!

Re-hydration is a major part of a player's performance and recovery process, and its importance is often overlooked. In many ways, it is more important for children to be aware of this (see Chapter 3).

Water is the main element of the body and needed for all vital functions. For soccer players, drinking plain water is not the most effective way to hydrate, therefore drinks should contain moderate levels of sodium and possibly some potassium. There are many sports drinks on the market which provide this. You should also make your players aware of this. During a moderate to high intensity workout in warm conditions I conducted a controlled experiment (unknown to the players) in which I offered them either water or a commercial drink. Seventy per cent chose water, these players assuming incorrectly that water was the most effective option.

Re-hydration tips

* Never drink until you are bloated.

* Thirst is not a good indication of dehydration.

* Replenish lost fluids within 12 hours of a match, if possible.

* Drink before, during and after training.

* Drink little and often.

* When not exercising, fluid should still be consumed in a variety of liquids such as fruit juice, semi-skimmed milk, low-sugar soft drinks and, of course, water.

* It is not good to consume alcohol after a game. Alcohol is a diuretic, which means it will increase the problem of dehydration. I have been advised that drinking 1 pint of beer must eventually be replaced by 1.25 pints of water!

Warning signs of dehydration

• Dark urine, possible strong smell.

• Heat intolerance.

• Flushed skin.

• Fatigue.

• Light-headedness.

• Loss of appetite.

Generally, for each kilogram of weight lost during exercise, at least 1.5 litres of fluid should be consumed to restore balance. This should be done within a reasonable period.

Team performance – Premiership 4–4–2 formation (Small sample only available)			
Left			**Right**
DC 10.02km	DC 10.02km	DC 10.02km	DC 10.79km
HI 962m	HI 610m	HI 610m	HI 952m
SD 255m	SD 145m	SD 145m	SD 250m
DC 11.15km	DC 11.60km	DC 11.60km	DC 11.48km
HI 1116m	HI 934m	HI 934m	HI 1181m
SD 313m	SD 196m	SD 196m	SD 308m
	DC 10.47km	DC 10.47km	
	HI 927m	HI 927m	
	SD 242m	SD 242m	

Turning and changing directions

Finally, I would like to briefly mention turning and changing direction with reference to an actual match and designing your own drill. Soccer is a multi-directional and multi-paced game. It is interesting to note that recent research has shown that players (subject to variables) change direction up to a thousand times and turn up to 450 times in a match. When designing drills, depending on their aim, try to include turns and changes of direction (any turns and changes of direction make the physical aspect much harder).

LESSONS LEARNED FROM PROZONE

Over the last three years I have learned many valuable lessons working with Prozone. All the facts below are based on players who have been directly involved with the programme. These lessons are also relevant to the amateur game:

- Statistics are influenced by individual players' abilities and desire.
- Team physical performance is influenced by training methods, e.g. long sessions tend to mean more aerobic endurance and maybe tiredness, while short sharp sessions tend to mean more high intensity training.
- Time of year influences physical performance, i.e. start of season, hot conditions, etc.
- Pre-season competitive games (or lack of them) influence conditioning statistics at the beginning of the season.
- Once the season begins, the balance between rest and training becomes very important, i.e. if the priority is physical and not tactical, do not be afraid to rest players as this will enhance physical performance, especially at the end of the season.

- On a normal cycle of a week, if the priority is physical (not tactical), give players the Thursday off, as this will enhance physical performance on Saturday (tapering).
- Any player who misses a part of pre-season (one week or more) or friendly games (× 2) will be affected physically in the first game of the season.
- Speed training, speed endurance and sprint work do have a positive effect on the statistics.
- Generally, players perform better physically on an evening kick-off (subject to variables) than a 3pm kick-off, especially if they do not train on the day of the match. However, this may be different for amateur players who work during the day and then have a match in the evening.
- Much can be learned about players' attitudes by studying the statistics with and without possession of the ball.
- Centre backs' statistics are usually dictated by the physical performance of the opposition centre forwards.
- Players playing two games in three days are statistically down between 5 and 10% from the average.
- Despite some schools of thought, there seems to be very little physical difference between Premiership and Championship players' physical performances.
- When designing training drills, be aware that in a 90-minute game, the majority of players (apart from centre backs) are constantly on the move, jogging etc., for 35 minutes plus. The rest of the time they are walking, standing still, etc.
- Individual players' graphs are more erratic than the team graphs. Players who are dropped or injured for three or four games and then come back to the first team tend to play satisfactorily on their initial return, but then during the second and third game the statistics drop below average, before recovering to average or above.
- There seems to be little difference between first and second half physical performance (subject to the state of the game).

'You can never be totally fit. There is always something you can work on to make you a better conditioned player – and therefore a better player.'
Richard Naylor, over 300 Premiership and League appearances.

Basic Training Principles

There are many excellent books discussing conditioning components and basic training principles for peak performance. Rather than attempt to cram all that accumulated knowledge into this book, the following is a very brief overview of the theory on which I have based practice. This is intended to give you a clear idea of where my methodology is coming from.

Physical fitness involves a multitude of components. Once you have studied the demands of the game, you can break down the components, often referred to as building blocks:

- Speed.
- Strength.
- Stamina.
- Suppleness (i.e. flexibility).
- Skill.

Each of these factors will be considered in more detail below.

Speed
Having more speed and power than an opposition team can give you a huge advantage in matches. It can create goals and get you out of awkward situations. If used correctly it is simply a massive advantage to have. Therefore, I have dedicated a chapter to this (see chapter 4).

Strength
Muscular endurance. There are many means of achieving this. Basically, strength can be split into three components:
- Lower body strength.
- Upper body strength.
- Core strength.

It is a major factor in power development and injury prevention work. Some of my favourite methods of achieving strength include dynamic medicine ball and bungee (resistance) work, Swiss ball and free weights. I also use specialist training programmes such as Frappier and MVP shuttle equipment (a form of horizontal plyometrics).

Stamina
Physical endurance – the foundation of all fitness. The fitter you are aerobically (interval training), the more effectively oxygen will be absorbed into your

bloodstream, increasing your heart power, which increases blood flow and removes waste products. This includes aerobic and anaerobic work.

Suppleness

Flexibility and agility help reduce injuries and enhance performance. This element of fitness must not be ignored. Dynamic flexibility and yoga-style stretching improves flexibility.

Skill

You can be as quick, strong, fit and agile as an Olympic decathlon athlete, but if you cannot control or pass a ball, then you will not make it to the top in football.

Although skill is not technically a building block of conditioning, it has to be included or all of the above components become irrelevant. One question I continually ask players, coaches and managers is: 'What makes a good or top-class player?' The answer is often:

1. Desire and attitude.

2. Skill and ability.

3. Conditioning and coaching.

Therefore, I hope you can see the importance of skill in creating a top player.

Other important factors include:

- Nutrition – 'what you eat is what you are' and it affects performance.

- Psychology – a player's mental outlook: attitude, confidence, etc.

- Desire – how hungry a player is, how much do they want success, how far will they push themselves, how much are they willing to sacrifice?

- Variety – as the season goes on, this takes up more of a prominent role. It is the key to maintaining freshness over a season.

- RRRR – Rest, Recovery, Refuelling and Re-hydration.

All the conditioning components are equally important, but if I have to choose the two most important that really make that difference in a long season of constant games, they have to be stamina (**muscular** and **aerobic endurance**) and speed. Those are the two that should take priority, but do not ignore the other components.

TRAINING MYTH

'Resistance training is no good for fat burning.'

Lean muscle is more metabolically active, so the more you have, the more your body ticks over when at rest and fires up when at work. You thus discharge more energy and therefore achieve greater calorie combustion.

Training principles for each session

I have used these basic principles for 20 years in and out of football, and they have always given good results personally and for the players I have worked with. Note that the sessions below should be adapted, if necessary, to adjust to the length and intensity of any pre-football sessions. You may have to reduce the volume of work or give the players a longer break between sessions. Watch, monitor and talk to the players.

Frequency

The number of training sessions during a period of time. In the early season, I suggest a minimum of four sessions per week is required to see improvement. Maintenance could be two to three sessions per week.

Intensity

How hard the players train. This is a massive individual factor. Overload and progression must be planned.

Time

Refers to the amount of time spent in a session. This should reflect certain demands of the game, i.e. how long players sprint, perform at high intensity or are consistently jogging etc. in a game.

Type

The type of exercise which trains each component. This should include specifity and variety.

Now let's look at individuality, specifity, overload, reversibility and recovery. These are some of the basic training principles I have followed for many years and which form the bases of much of my training, especially strength and endurance work.

Individuality

Everyone is an individual subject to their own unique make-up. The needs of an individual player consist of position, age and profile (strength, weakness, opportunity and threat) and mentality.

Specifity

For the majority of the time, conditioning must be relevant to the game, i.e. with or without a ball, but it does not mean you ignore cross-training.

Overload

TRAIN → OVERLOAD → ADAPTS → REST → TRAIN AGAIN. Subject to each component, this is a simple way to show how overload should be progressive and structured.

Reversibility

This is the time period in which a player's fitness will regress back to the level at which they began training – for example, if a player trains well for six weeks and then stops, it might take only two weeks for them to lose the pace and strength built up over the previous six. It is interesting to note that, in my experience and analysis, speed is the first component players lose, with strength closely behind if they get injured.

Recovery/rest

The benefits of recovery for a fully fit player are highly underestimated. Constant analysis/testing has shown that players perform better (physically) before a test or a match if they have had two to three days off or have had their 'rest day' 48 hours before a match. Prozone has also shown that in 65% of evening kick-off matches players reach above-average statistics for physical performance if they do not train on the day and have a 32-hour break between the last training session and the match (see pages 26–7 concerning amateur players). This is subject to football variables. Recovery is also an important factor in training principles. The question arises: 'Does the priority lie in physical fitness (freshness) or in tactical, formation and skill issues as to what you do during a build-up to a match?' In other words, if you are happy with the tactics and formations and you want players to be as fresh as possible, give them the Thursday off before a Saturday kick-off. Ultimately, this will probably be the manager's decision if you are conditioning professional players.

2 PLANNING TRAINING FOR THE SEASON

This chapter will consider the importance of planning training for the team in a yearly cycle. It will look at the key points of planning, the benefits, the factors that influence planning, and the cycles in a soccer season, and how these can affect amateur and young players.

Planning your team's training should fall into four key phases and these will form the basis of the chapter:

- Close season.

- Pre-season.

- Early/in-season.

- Maintenance period.

TRAINING BRIEF – PSYCHOLOGY OF SOCCER

Psychology is an area in which soccer has come a long way, and which is now an integral part of the game, though much more remains to be done to improve the mental strength of players and coaches.

I am not going to attempt to explain this area in detail, but I am aware of its importance in football overall, at whatever level of soccer you play. It is an untapped and highly under-trained area. For me, this is summed up in Jerry Lynch's book, *Creative Coaching*, where he states: 'It takes time to train the mind; like a muscle, the mind needs to be stretched and exercised daily if you want to develop it and make it strong.' A high degree of discipline is required to apply this.

In my experience, some players accept the mental aspect of the game, some do not want to know, some just go through the motions and nothing else, and some are open-minded, so you may have to use different approaches. This can also just as easily apply to coaches. Conditioning coaches need to have an open mind, as this will make them a better coach. I once heard the phrase, 'In an open mind there are many possibilities, in an expert mind there are few!'

For me, success in the game involves mental strength, the will to win, being positive most of the time, and nurturing confidence and desire. Let me quote Frank Dick, who to me summarises perfectly the part psychology plays in giving an advantage: 'It is mental power that separates the exceptional from the very good. When they line up for the race there will be nothing to choose between them, talent for talent, training for training. What separates them is what goes on behind the eyes.'

I have had experience of players' fitness and their psychological state. For example, if you tell players they are looking tired, they tend to act as though they are tired. If you tell players that their test results are the best they have ever been, they seem to have more reserve running power in them. The most important lesson I have learned is that a winning and happy team tends to have fewer injuries than a losing and unhappy team!

Why Plan?

Planning is absolutely essential – it sets the standards that you expect from your players early on, and will provide strong foundations for the team's performance during the season. Any team, adults and juniors alike, needs to have a clear conditioning plan if they have any form of pre-season training or if they train between matches. In other words, any team that wants to do well *must* plan.

The plan is essential because it will allow you to:

- Develop a balanced programme.
- Vary training loads throughout the season.
- Aid Rest, Recovery, Refuelling and Re-hydration.
- Achieve peak performance, week in, week out.
- Look after vulnerable individuals.
- Achieve variety when required.
- Avoid overtraining and burnout.

The importance of planning is obvious when you see it written down, but is often overlooked, particularly by managers who have to juggle other priorities. If, in your capacity as coach, you find yourself in this situation, then it is your duty to champion the cause of long-term planning of training. Sure, it may take time now – planning for a whole season is not a simple task – but it *will* head off problems in the future; the sort of problems that you won't want to deal with in the middle of the season.

There's a classic saying in project management and it should be the mantra for any conditioning coach: 'Failing to plan is planning for failure.' Effective player conditioning is not achieved overnight and it does not happen by itself. It is a gradual process taking weeks and months before you and the team begin to see the results. When working with children and young players it can take years of careful planning and training to get the players to where they need to be.

Influencing factors

There are many factors that will influence your planning, such as games, results, the morale of the players (these factors rarely exist in isolation and are often inter-linked). For example, the team may be on a losing streak and as a result morale may be low. If this is the case you may want to change the training that you are doing to freshen things up and break the routine. You need to be aware of the factors which influence your planning and be prepared to change your plans; just because you have committed your plan to paper does not mean that it cannot be changed.

Factors that may influence your season planning include:

- The manager's requirements.
- Your goals and aims (see below).
- Past performance and current fitness levels.
- Fixtures and fixture congestion.
- International weekends – for those lucky few!
- Cup competitions.
- Facilities.
- Time of year.
- Realism – design a plan which you can keep to.

In contrast, factors that may lead you to changing your plans include:

- Fitness testing – what are the results telling you?
- Feedback from the players.
- Morale of the players.
- Weather conditions.
- Re-arranged fixtures.
- Manager's requirements (these invariably change as the season progresses).
- League position of the club.
- Results on the pitch (although in an ideal world this should not influence the conditioning plan).

Give particular attention to the players – they can soon get bored. If possible, be sure to change the location of training and the methods that you use to keep the players interested. Remember to work with the manager – every manager and coach has their own views and ways of doing things; it's essential that you work as a partnership.

Planning for special groups
Individuals
Planning for the season usually happens at the team level, but you also need to bear in mind certain types of individual, e.g. young players, seniors, injury-prone players and international players. These are all specialised groups and will need specific programmes that fit into your overall conditioning plan.

For more information of the specific requirements of individuals according to the position they play etc. see Chapter 1.

> 'Football is a game for athletes. Whether we like it or not, if you can't run, you can't play.'
>
> *Joe Royle, former England international,*
> *1,000 games as Premiership and League manager*

Amateur football
Relatively few coaches have the luxury of full-time players and the freedom that this gives when planning. With semi-professional and amateur football you have one major stumbling block when it comes to planning and conditioning – time (or the lack of it). If you only get one or two hours a week to train, most of that time must be spent on skills or technical points, but spending 15–25 minutes on a conditioning component can only be good for the individual and the team.

Generally speaking, the higher up the non-league ladder you are, the less of a problem the time component should be and the more important conditioning should be (and the more training sessions you have).

Most Saturday and Sunday players train perhaps once during the week, and conditioning tends to be seen as a secondary issue. Conditioning is often left to the individual, but this does not mean that planning is less important – if anything it increases its importance. With just a few minutes each week you have to make clear what it is you expect from your players and send them off with no doubts as to what they must do during the week, on their own initiative. There's never an excuse to ignore planning!

As you will see on page 28, the starting point for the plan is always to set the goal. So, start by getting each player to ask themselves the question, 'Why do I play?' Is it social, is it for fun, is it to win, is it to improve, or is it just to keep in shape?

If it is either of the first two reasons, then fine; your job is to ensure that the player has a basic foundation of fitness so they can enjoy the game and not get injured or suffer too much the next day. If it is the latter three reasons, then a bit of planning, week to week, will help the player to achieve their (and your) objectives.

When planning at this level, try to get your players to follow some of these tips:
• Something is better then nothing.
• Try to train with a team-mate or friend.
• Train in the early part of the week.
• Be sensible and safe.
• Be position specific to what you do, e.g. a centre back and a midfielder require totally different programmes.
• The fitter you are, the better you will perform and be able to help your team-mates.
• Try to avoid running on pavements and tarmac (softer surfaces such as grass are much more forgiving on the body).
• Try to make it enjoyable; for example, I once suggested squash to a very tall and well built centre back who needed to improve his footwork and reaction time.

If you are fortunate enough to train two or three evenings a week, then planning is important not only to improve team conditioning and to give the team that elusive edge, but it also prevents burnout and fatigue. In this situation, you should be pushing for a full programme of conditioning, giving special consideration to pre-season training which is often overlooked at this level.

Children and young adults
Planning for children and young adults is almost the opposite of planning for adult amateur players – time is on your side. In fact, you have years to develop the separate components of conditioning.

Young players will not be fully physically developed until their late teens or early twenties, so enjoyment of the game must be the main priority. Planning for conditioning takes a less important role; generally speaking, well organised soccer training will allow younger players to improve their fitness.

Some of the components of conditioning are not relevant (for example, stamina will be achieved by just playing soccer) so you should concentrate on components like running techniques (speed), body movement, SAQ (speed, agility and quickness) work, suppleness, and basic techniques for strength work, thereby laying the foundations for the future.

The older children get, the more relevant planning becomes to improve conditioning components and to avoid injury and burnout. It may seem that with more time and fewer areas of conditioning to be concerned about, planning for this group is less of an issue. Think again. It becomes more important; not only do you need to plan the season for the team, but you also need to plan for individuals as they grow and mature at different rates. Keep an eye on the years ahead and how your plans now will affect the future. Added to this, with some areas of conditioning off limits, e.g. weights work, you have the additional task of keeping training fresh but with fewer drills to choose from.

It is interesting to note that recent analysis (over a two-year period) shows that when a boy goes through a growth spurt (growing several centimetres over a few months) this tends to affect his performance during training and matches, and may make him injury prone.

In short, no matter what team you are responsible for, planning is your first duty!

'Listen to your body – you know when you're tired, and you know when you need to work hard. Be honest with yourself and your team-mates.'

Tommy Miller, over 300 Premiership and League appearances

Putting the plan together

Before you put pen to paper and begin to formulate the training plan for your team, you must first ask yourself what it is you are trying to achieve; at the end of the season what will you, as the conditioning coach, see as success for your plan? It sounds a simple question, but give it some thought and the answers are not so obvious.

Let me give you a couple of examples. After carrying out a simple SWOT (strength, weakness, opportunities and threats) with the Under-15 and Under-14 teams, it was decided by all as a team, not individuals, that they needed strengthening work. The goal was set to get stronger by 20% or more. Therefore we put a programme together for the children to do at home, in their own time (only 15 minutes three or four times a week) and did one session a week at the training ground. The programme was a one-year plan, with the first cycle concentrating on core stability, the second cycle on technique, the third cycle on work against their own body weight and subsequent cycles progressively overloading them.

The second example is with our first team. At the beginning of the season we knew we had a chance of making the play-offs, which could potentially increase the season by a month (in previous seasons our physical performances may have suffered at the end of the season; see pages 7–8). We therefore decided to protect the players as much as possible by monitoring and making the 4Rs (Rest, Recovery, Refuelling and Re-hydration) a priority in the last few cycles, and not being afraid to give the players time off (so our goal was to ensure our physical performance did not dip at the end of the season).

Here are some things to bear in mind when planning conditioning for the season:

- A plan should be put in place during the close season.
- There should be a goal/aim.
- It should be agreed by the manager, coaches and fitness conditioners.
- The plan should be over one full season, including close season.
- Use fixtures (when available) and weekends off to assist your plan.
- Divide the plan into periods or cycles. For example, divide the season into four macro-cycles each of three months' duration, and then further divide into meso-cycles (six to eight weeks) and micro-cycles (one or two weeks). Each period should have specific goals and aims.

The planning cycle

When planning a season, there are four key periods:

1. **Close season period** – to initially ensure rest (both physical and mental) and then maintenance. May and June.
2. **Pre-season period** – building the conditioning components and pre-season friendlies. July to mid-August.
3. **Early/in-season period** – improving some or all conditioning components. This period can be further divided. September to December.
4. **Maintenance period** – maintain improvements and continue to improve certain conditioning components. This period can be further divided. January to end of season.

From this basic structure you can develop a more detailed plan, which includes additional phases in the in-season and maintenance periods. The following can be used as a starting point for your planning, but remember it does not take any of the influences and other points described above into account.

The periods or cycles described are normally six to eight weeks, and within these cycles you will have your normal weekly routine (sometimes referred to as the micro-cycles). Although this plan has been designed for a professional team, you can still follow these guidelines if you work with amateur or younger players, as it is appropriate for all teams that train. However, for children, remember that the priority must be enjoyment.

This plan has been developed to accommodate a 50+ match season, lasting eight to nine months, with hectic periods during August, December and April.

Note that the dates are only a rough guide.

Close season period

Dates: 6 May – 1 July

The close season has a direct impact on pre-season (which in my view is the most important cycle in conditioning). Despite this, it is the part of the year that is overlooked by many coaches.

This close season period lasts for anything between five weeks to eight weeks, depending on circumstances. Some coaches suggest maintaining fitness by working throughout this period, but I do not totally agree. In my experience, it should be a period sub-divided into three smaller phases of:

• Complete physical and mental rest (apart from stretching routine).

• Active rest phase.

• Preparation phase.

Over a season that lasts for nine to ten months, the body will take a pounding, both physically and mentally. There are not many sports where you are expected to physically peak for 40–50 games a season and train hard between them! Bodies are not machines; knocks, strains and mental tiredness accumulated during a season can create injuries and lead to under-performance. It is necessary to give minds a break and a chance for bodies to recuperate. Another consideration, as our analysis shows, is that players do not lose any aerobic fitness if they stop training for a period of 10–28 days (so long as the individual player keeps active using other activities such as swimming and cycling). For amateur players this period could be less, maybe 10–14 days.

Amateur players

For amateur players, the close season depends on how high you are in the non-league ladder. Basically, the higher you are, the more you should follow the professional players' programme. If you are a weekend player, and depending on why you play (see page 27), you should loosely adhere to it, bearing in mind two main considerations. After the initial complete rest phase (see page 31) you should try to maintain your conditioning by perhaps entering the team in local five-a-side tournaments or leagues. This is fun, but it also helps maintain your skills, sharpness and conditioning. Secondly, get the players to participate in some other sports (cross-training), such as squash, tennis, badminton, etc., to maintain their conditioning levels. Remember, the lower you are in the amateur leagues, the less time you have to prepare as a team, especially during the pre-season cycle.

Children and young players
For children, the close season should mainly be about giving their bodies and minds a rest, giving the soccer muscles a break, and even trying different sports to maintain their conditioning. The younger the player is, the more immature their body, therefore rest is very important; remember, for the coach and player, time is on your side.

Complete physical and mental rest
Apart from stretching routines, encourage the players to have complete rest – tell them to get away from football, refrain from watching any football on television, enjoy a holiday, and take part in light physical activity such as walking or playing golf. This period should last approximately two to three weeks, depending on the individual. Rest – physical and mental – takes priority at this stage of the season.

Active rest period
This is a period designed to maintain certain levels of fitness through non-football-related activities such as swimming, tennis, cycling, squash or even gym work. Again, this should last for two to three weeks and players should be working at a moderate level.

Preparation phase
The preparation phase for pre-season lasts about 7–14 days. It is a structured programme of conditioning and rest. Conditioning includes core stability, stretching, strength work and aerobic interval training on grass or treadmill surfaces. Players are now working at moderate to high levels but under a structured schedule of work – work one day, rest the next. This phase is designed with intensity levels as the key, depending on how you expect the players to return physically (what condition they are in).

Finally, the days of players returning to pre-season overweight and with an increased percentage of body fat have nearly ended (especially in the top levels of amateur and professional football). Fitness conditioning and soccer coaches' knowledge and professionalism have increased a player's awareness of this problem, but there are still some who lack self-discipline and return to the season overweight. These players must be treated individually and given a separate programme to lose weight and get fit before joining their team-mates. My analysis has shown a direct connection between overweight and badly conditioned players and injuries sustained during pre-season, especially Achilles and calf injuries.

Pre-season period

Dates: 1 July–10 August

Pre-season is one of the most important periods of the season, lasting approximately six weeks, depending on circumstances. It is not only the foundation of fitness conditioning, but is also about setting standards of conditioning, tactics, skills, attitudes and discipline for the forthcoming season. It can also be a great measure of the hunger and desire of the players, and shows which players have looked after themselves (close season) and how hard they can push themselves at the appropriate time (pre-season). It is the period in which I have seen players who were not in the previous year's regular starting eleven catch the eye of the manager and the coaches, become regulars in the team and then go on to greater things. I have also observed a connection between players who become injured during pre-season and the lack of both fitness and playing form in the early part of the season.

> **TRAINING BRIEF – WARM-UP**
>
> Warm-ups are basically designed to prepare players for a training session or game so they train or play optimally and avoid injury. Try to vary warm-up sessions on a day-to-day basis, without leaving out the basic principles. One of the most successful ways to vary warm-ups is to get different coaches or conditioners to supervise them, thereby helping to keep players interested. This promotes the mental side of a warm-up. It is important to get the players thinking, getting them bright and alert before practice. This can be done by word, letter or number games, or general knowledge questions (short question, short answers), for example, a simple adding-up game. The coach chooses a number, say eleven; as the players are doing their warm-up, he chooses a player and says four. The player, with no hesitation, must say seven (4 + 7 =11). If he hesitates or gets it wrong, five press-ups.

This cycle/period is again split into three separate phases:

- Initial phase.
- Friendlies, and strength, power and speed phase.
- Quality over quantity phase.

For me, pre-season is the period that has to be planned with complete accuracy to ensure that come the first match of the season, the players are physically ready. If the foundations are not laid correctly, the conditioning of the players will eventually start to show cracks and crumble!

One thing to remember: the shorter the close season cycle, the less conditioning is required during the pre-season. For example, if your players only have four to five weeks off in the close season, less conditioning is required in the pre-season as the reversibility factor will have had less time to take effect (i.e. players will have lost less of their base fitness). However, if players have eight to nine weeks off during the close season, conditioning during the pre-season becomes highly important. As I mentioned earlier, the close season cycle very much dictates what happens in the pre-season.

> **TRAINING MYTH**
>
> 'The only way to burn fat is to work out at the so called "fat-burning" zone for long durations.'
>
> This subject is much debated. Fat can be burned at any exercise intensity up to around 90% of maximum heart rate. Basically, any exercise burns fat (how much depends on intensity, which is the prominent factor rather than duration of exercise taken). For training and games we tend to work at a moderate to high intensity level. Sometimes working at a low intensity for a longer period 'rests' the more prominent high intensity energy systems, therefore a fat-burning workout can be done without affecting normal training.

Amateur players

Time is a major factor for the majority of players and therefore much work needs to be done by the individual. The importance of pre-season does not diminish just because you are an amateur; in fact, it is probably more important because the fitness levels/standards vary so much between teams. Fitter individuals and teams have the advantage, especially at the end of a game. The more you can do (safely), the better player you will become. Use the plan/overview as a general guideline to what levels to work to, when to rest, what to prioritise, etc.

I have seen and been involved with many amateur teams (average standard Saturday and Sunday teams that train once or twice a week during pre-season) which train too hard in the early part of this cycle/period, causing many injuries and de-motivating players to the extent that turnout for the next sessions decreases.

This is why planning is important to ensure this does not happen; by planning you can find out which players cannot make the team sessions and try to persuade them to do some training by themselves or with a friend. Remember, you can always advise them on what type of training to do. Something is better than nothing.

Children and young players

The younger the child is, the less relevant this is. In general terms, for pre-growth children the pre-season period is not really relevant. With post-growth children, this period can be used to lay down simple foundation work, such as stretching routines, core strength work, running techniques (mechanics) and basic strength and power work. A certain amount of cardiovascular (aerobic) work can also be done, ideally with a ball (the younger you are, the more relevant it is to do this with a ball).

The initial phase

This usually consists of two weeks, to ease players back into all aspects of conditioning under controlled circumstances. Emphasis is on core stability, strength and stretching, very basic speed and power techniques and drills, but mainly aerobic (and some anaerobic) endurance work. Field tests are carried out during the end of this phase as they will tell you the physical shape of the players, with plenty of time before the season starts, should you need to change your plans. We measure aerobic fitness (bleep test, 12-minute run, VO2 Max) and basic strength (core, squats, lunges, etc.).

Initial friendly matches, and the strength, power and speed phase

The initial friendly match should involve all team members playing only 45 minutes of the first game, against moderate opposition. Between friendlies and rest/recovery phases, continue with speed, power and all round strength work. This phase lasts for two weeks and ideally you would expect players to play two further 90-minute games after the initial 45-minute match.

The quality rather than quantity phase

This lasts for a further two weeks. It consists of two or three quality competitive matches to assist sharpness. This is the phase when conditioning is worked around matches. Testing also continues. It is a high intensity conditioning period, short and sharp. At the end of this phase, do not be afraid to rest players before the first match of the competitive season. Do lots of speed work and speed endurance. Individual programmes start.

Key points for conditioning during pre-season

When taking the team through pre-season I have found that bearing the following points in mind helps me to get the most out of this critical part of the year.

- **Player preparation** – Ensure that players follow their guidelines during the close season. Explain to them the benefits of following the programme and let them know the consequences of coming back overweight or with a high body fat percentage (depending on the standard of the soccer being played).

- **Coach preparation** – This is the only cycle in the year where results will not affect the training plan. Look at the team, but remember to give consideration to individuals' needs. Work with the football coaches to include conditioning, with or without the ball, as part of the overall plan.

- **Doing too much too quickly** – Implement a gradual build-up of all the components of fitness. Do not be afraid to start gradually. The continuous testing will indicate each player's physical state. Remember, there is no substitute for good competitive pre-season friendlies to improve players' conditioning and sharpness at the end of the pre-season phase.

- **Concentrate on basic fitness components** – Pre-season should be about increasing aerobic endurance and developing core stability and all-round strength. This will lay the foundation for a long season and for the more intense training to come.

- **Plan friendlies for first** and reserve teams with correct recovery and rest days – Do not fit in too many games too quickly. Try to plan the reserve games (first-teamers who do not get a game with the first eleven) the day after the first-team game. This will assist training between games and help coaches to have a first-team squad to train with between games. If going on tour, avoid cramming in too many games. Ideally, you want to play two games in five days.

- **Too much travelling** – Avoid long-distance away games and tours that require a great deal of travelling between games. This can be a reason why away performances are sometimes below par.

- **Use swimming** – Get the players in the pool for recovery sessions and also use the pool for aerobic and anaerobic conditioning sessions. Even non-swimmers can work hard in swimming pools if you are well organised, for example, jogging in the pool with high knee lifts, or swimming with the aid of floats.

And finally . . .

- Put the science into practice that makes an impact and makes sense, e.g. if you only have half a dozen sessions of two hours each and then the season starts, concentrate on aerobic endurance.

- Dehydration levels; weigh players before and after training to show fluid loss. This is a great exercise for amateur and young players which they won't forget. See page 14.

- The surfaces you train on; avoid road running or very hard surfaces for long sessions. Try to train on grass as much as possible.

- Training should be realistic to the demands of the game; see chapter 1.

- Players' footwear. Measure the players' feet; trainers should be the right type, size and width. They are not a fashion statement. In my experience, correctly fitting footwear reduces injuries significantly.

- Research has shown that Achilles tendons may shrink or contract very slightly during close season, therefore have a good plan in place for stretching.
- Variety – cross-training, different locations and voices. This will help to keep the training fresh and interesting.
- What and when do you test? See Chapter 5.
- Know your players' heart rate maximum. If you are going to use heart rate monitors make sure you know what you are doing, and ensure you have enough.
- When you can, treat players as individuals, depending on their position. There will be times, especially as the season progresses, when certain conditioning drills may be position-specific, e.g. strength work for centre backs and aerobic endurance for midfielders.
- Try to include your youth/Academy teams (16/17-year-olds+) with the first team, not for all the drills, but some sessions (speed drills). This will help both sets of players integrate.
- Work with the physios on inner core work, stretching, injury prevention and strength work, etc.
- Sell the benefits of pre-season conditioning to the players. Get everybody to agree the same goal and aim.
- International players need to be treated differently; they need rest (if they are to play for their country at the end of the season).

> 'Rest is important and is part of any good training programme. Mental strength is very important, especially in pre-season. If you believe you can do a run, you will. If you don't, you won't.'
>
> *Gavin Williams, Wales international, over 300 League appearances*

Overview of a pre-season plan

I hope that it has become obvious that planning must be carried out according to the specific circumstances that you find yourself in – there's no one plan that fits all. However, starting with a blank piece of paper and attempting to plan your season can be a daunting project, so here are a few plans that I have used in recent years. They all cover the pre-season, as this is where the conditioning coach really has to deliver the goods – it's vital for the rest of the season.

There are three plans:

1. Pre-season summary sheet – this covers the four simple aims of conditioning in pre-season.

2. Overview – this is the overview sheet for a whole pre-season cycle, day by day. Please see Appendix 1 on pages 157–9 for full plan.

3. Detailed plan – this is a detailed look at the first week of pre-season training. Please see Appendix 2 on pages 160–1 for full plan.

When you come to your own planning, try to make each pre-season different, whether by changing the drills, locations or coaches. Avoid the temptation to get last season's plan out of the drawer, dust it down and use it again – the players will remember it!

Summary sheet

I always carry this in my pocket during pre-season to remind me of the core components that we need to work on at this stage. It's a really useful prompt and ensures I stay focused and do not get distracted. It lays out my goals and aims during this period and reminds me all the time of what I want to achieve. It is also a useful tool to show soccer coaches, and even players if they have any queries!

INCREASE VO2 MAX	SPEED and POWER
Recovery training (H/R monitors)	anaerobic { speed training / speed endurance
Low } Moderate } aerobic High intensity	Bungee work and Frappier system Basic plyometrics
PROACTIVE INJURY PREVENTION	**TESTING**
• Core stability • Dynamic stretching • Wobble board • Muscle strength-specific	Bleep test x 2 Treadmill test 12min test T-agility speed test 5.20–25m sprint tests – rolling starts, etc.

Overview

The overview summarises the progressive overloading of the players, day by day, during this period. It is useful to have this close by you in case of unforeseen circumstances that may mean you have to change a drill or session that may affect the next day's training, e.g. swimming pool suddenly becomes unavailable, or the training pitches are unplayable, or weather is a factor.

Week 1						
M	T	W	T	F	S	S
Stadium/ Park	Stadium/ Park	RAF location	RAF location	Training		
10.00am Park: Runs + Strength Work	10.00am Gym: Runs + Strength Work	9.30am Interval Training + Strength Work + Pool	9.30am Interval Training + Strength Work + Pool	9.30am Testing; Strength Work + Head Tennis	OFF	OFF
4.00pm Training Ground Soccer	4.00pm Training Ground Soccer	pm off	4.00pm Soccer	pm off		
LOW	LOW/ MOD	MOD	MOD/ HIGH	MOD		

Detailed plan

This plan adds detail to the overall schedule for pre-season above. I have included just the first week of pre-season to illustrate the approach that I take. Over the next five weeks I continue testing the players and the emphasis gradually switches to the speed and power components of conditioning. Aerobic fitness will be maintained and improved by playing matches.

Give the manager, coaches and physio a copy of the plan. Work out the progression, overloading, cross-training and recovery in detail. For me, if I do a session or a plan, I try to visualise it in my head to see if it's going to work. At times I will even try it myself.

Week 1				
Monday	10.00am	Stadium/ Park	6mins jog/stretches	Low intensity
			12mins jog; dynamic stretches	
			3 groups (rotate after 5 mins and 10 mins): Group 1: basic agility work Group 2: basic multi-direction work Group 3: basic speed work	
			Stretches; 6mins jog	
			40mins basic core stability, wobble board work, all-round strength work (dyno bands, medicine ball etc., 4 x physios)	
	4.00pm	Training ground	45mins basic soccer work with coaches	Low intensity

It should be noted that this plan was put together in conjunction with our club physios who have their own progressive plan for all strength work, core stability, wobble board, medicine balls and dyno bands. If you do not have a physio's resources available, doing basic strength work such as press-ups, sit-ups, dorsi raisers, squats, standing on one leg to work your balance, lunges etc. would be an alternative. For a very basic example see the drill 31 on page 118.

For amateur players, depending how many evenings or weekend days you have available, try to do at least one running drill and some strength work for each session you do. Due to lack of time, try to condense the running sessions to 25 minutes and the strength work to 10–15 minutes. The rest of the session should be spent on soccer.

TRAINING MYTH
'Weight training makes you slow.'
Tell that to Maurice Greene or Justin Gatlin. Weight training relies on short-term energy systems and your fast twitch fibres. It does not take a rocket scientist to work out that fast, safe weightlifting makes you a quicker athlete.

Summary
Close and pre-season success or failure is generally judged by the results the team has at the beginning of the season. This is wrong. There are so many other influential factors that are out of the conditioner's control. Although fitness conditioning is a very important component of the overall picture, it is just one of the several components which make a winning/losing team. However, this is indicative of the business we are in, so we have to accept it.

I believe that close and pre-season success or failure, in terms of conditioning, should be based on test results, the number of injuries (or lack of them) and the players' attitudes and freshness at the time of the first competitive game of the season.

Remember the goal that we set down at the beginning of this book: 'The ability to compete in a game of football for its entire duration with fitness/conditioning being a positive component, win, draw or lose'.

Early/in-season period
Dates: September–January

Amateur and professional players
This consists of three separate cycles (see page 41) for variety. The general goal and aim of this long period is to continue to improve players' conditioning. For professional players, follow the guidelines below, bearing in mind that you work with them every day, and therefore you know their strengths and weaknesses and can tailor more intense training to certain individuals.

First of all, you need a simple written plan for this period which, as mentioned above, is split into three cycles. By having this plan, you can see the past, present and future, which in my opinion helps you to adjust to any unforeseen circumstances like weather, pitch condition, players' attitude and physical state, etc. If there is an unforeseen problem, missing or changing a session is not a disaster, just re-adjust.

We can see how this would work more practically by using speed as the example. The goal for this long period is to improve players' speed. Because it is a long period, use the three separate cycles to continually overload and improve the players by varying each cycle. The first cycle may be developing the power base (gym, Frappier or bungee work), the second cycle may be working anticipation, reaction and the golden step rule. The final cycle may be doing SAQ work (foot-to-ground contact and technique).

When dealing with injured players who have been out for a couple of weeks, putting them back in the programme should not be a problem (with professionals, even being out for three or four weeks should not create a problem, although common sense needs to be applied). For longer periods of injury, players must be treated on an individual basis with aerobic conditioning (stamina) being the priority.

With new players arriving at your club the first thing you should do is assess their conditioning by:

- Talking to the player about his current state of conditioning.
- Finding out how many games he has played.
- Asking for any previous injury history.
- Asking for any previous test results.
- Carrying out some basic testing, if required.

All this will give you the picture you require to decide whether to put him straight into the current programme.

TRAINING BRIEF – REST

As the season progresses, especially the last few cycles, rest becomes extremely important (matches and sharp training sessions will maintain the players' conditioning, if they are playing regularly). If the players are not fit by this stage of the season, then it is too late. Physical rest and mental rest are two separate issues, but are connected.

I was once told, 'Everything will eventually catch you up physically' and working with the first team for eight years I have seen many examples of this in the form of illness, loss of form, declining conditioning statistics, lack of motivation, injuries, etc. Sometimes it takes just a few weeks or months, but on other occasions it can take a cycle of two years.

By knowing the players and talking to them, and through the testing and monitoring protocols, you can be proactive instead of reactive. At times the conditioner will have to be assertive with managers and coaches, which he must be for the benefit of the players. In other words, don't be afraid to give players a rest.

Mental tiredness manifests itself in lack of motivation, desire, enthusiasm, etc. It is important, if possible, to give players and coaches time away from each other. I have heard many times how, when teams are struggling, they seem to work harder and longer. In my opinion, this is wrong. Training should be balanced, ensuring players have time away from each other to help keep things fresh, and not be stuck in the same old routine. Change training locations; occasionally consider introducing different coaches.

Children and young players

Much of the above applies to children and young players, especially the structure. The main difference, as already mentioned, is that you have more time – not just one season, but several. You will also have to start at a lesser intensity, e.g., strength work, the three cycles could be;

1. Core.

2. Strength (against his own body).

3. SAQ and technique.

You must never forget that with children it's all about fun, enjoyment and even falling in love with the game, especially if you are dealing with young children.

The cycles
Early season cycle
Dates: 10 August–25 September

As the season gets under way you should be looking for final improvement in match fitness and sharpness. Be sure to continue testing and monitoring. Individual programmes should also start to progress at this stage.

If you are working on a specific component that takes two cycles/periods, for example, speed and power over early- and into-season cycles, it is important that you change the method you are using to keep the sessions fresh and full of variety. In this example, in the early cycle you may use Frappier sessions (see page 109) and change this to bungee sessions (see page 127) during the into-season cycle.

Into-season cycle

Dates: 25 September–7 November

Continue with speed components and individual requirements. Keep assessing aerobic fitness.

Winter season cycle

Dates: 7 November–Christmas

Pitches start to become heavy, causing possible injuries, such as Achilles, calf, and hamstring injuries. At this stage of the season another cycle of testing may be required to ensure that conditioning levels are correct. Speed is still prominent. At the end of this period, conditioning becomes a maintenance component, rather than a developmental one, due to the hectic Christmas schedule and number of matches played.

Christmas period

Dates: 22 December–7 January

Due to the schedule of fixtures, ease off all conditioning; the 4Rs (rest, recovery, refuelling and re-hydration) are your priority. Pool sessions are used, also days off.

Maintenance period

Early maintenance cycle

Dates: 7 January–20 February

At this time of the year, the weather may affect training. Start introducing variety and cross training to the programme – conditioning is short and sharp with maintenance the key. Football training should maintain aerobic fitness.

Late maintenance cycle

Dates: 20 February–early April

This is the time of the season you may get fatigue or overtraining-related injuries, or some players even becoming lethargic towards their training. Conditioning is reduced at this stage – avoid long training sessions and add cross-training once a week. This *may* be the final cycle of testing.

Easter to end-of-season cycle

Dates: mid-April to end of season

Short, sharp sessions of football are required. Attitude, motivation and fatigue become big issues and variety is important. In an ideal world, there would be a de-training week (gradual reduction of physical training, or several days of warm-down and stretching) as the teams winds down from conditioning. However, it may not be a priority!

Amateur and professional players

For these players the maintenance period usually lasts from January to April/May, and again consists of three separate cycles to give variety (see page 42). The general goal is to maintain conditioning levels without fatigue, overtraining and boredom becoming an issue, especially in the later cycles. Also, variety and cross-training become important (with professionals, this phase is even more important because they are more intense than amateurs).

Overload to maintain, not to improve, is an important principle, although this is not easy to achieve unless you talk to the players and do some basic testing only. Here are some of my golden rules for this phase:

- Try to treat the players as individuals. Some might need to work harder than others or rest more than others.
- Avoid long training sessions which could lead to fatigue and overtraining injuries.
- Introduce variety and cross-training.
- Soccer training, short and sharp, should help maintain conditioning.
- Try to train at different locations if possible.
- Don't be afraid to give players time off.
- Try to make training a bit more fun.
- Perhaps get other coaches to do a session.
- Five-a-side competitions are always popular.
- Basic testing only required at the start of the cycle.
- Talk to the players.

Children and young players

Although the principles above should apply, the maintenance period for children and younger players should, in my opinion and experience, kick in a bit later (about February to March), for two main reasons: the intensity with the children is less than with adults (and more fun with children) and you are trying to develop a long term plan of several years.

Therefore my golden rules should apply in the last cycle, March–April time.

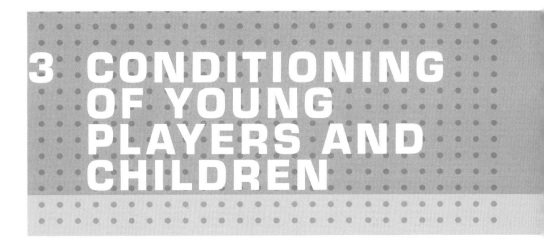

3 CONDITIONING OF YOUNG PLAYERS AND CHILDREN

This chapter will look at the specifics of conditioning young players and children, i.e. juniors from 9–18 years old. It will look at what you need to know as coach about the physical development of children and also give guidance on the conditioning tests that are suitable for this group of players.

This chapter will cover:
- Why we need to consider children and young adults as a specific group when planning conditioning.
- Some interesting analysis from the Academy at Ipswich.
- An overview of the three keys groups of young players (for the purposes of conditioning).
- What you need to know as a coach before you begin to develop a conditioning programme for young players.
- Setting a conditioning programme for young players.
- A range of tests that can be used to monitor the conditioning of young players and benchmark results.

SAFETY AND WELFARE OF CHILDREN

As managers, coaches and conditioners – indeed, whatever your involvement with junior football – you have a duty of care towards young players (those under 18 years of age) whilst they are under your supervision. Of course, this is a moral responsibility, but it is also worth remembering that this is also a legal duty. You should ensure that everyone can take part in an enjoyable and safe environment – the aim is to create a culture and atmosphere in which children and young people can have fun and take part safely.

There are a number of best practices and guidelines available from both the FA and the NSPCC, covering issues such as abuse, bullying, equal opportunities and discrimination. I would also recommend you attend the FA workshop on Child Protection and Best Practices. Even if it is only for peace of mind, it is well worth the time invested.

Conditioning for Children and Young Adults

I have had the privilege of working with children and young adults since the early nineties through the community scheme as an FA coach and since the mid-nineties as a conditioning adviser to the Youth Team System at Ipswich Town. This chapter is based on my personal experience of the past 15 years, and the knowledge and understanding of the basic theory of the physiology of children and young adults I have gained.

'You know your body, you work with your body, you know how far you can push yourself, it's just a matter of applying yourself. Mental strength.'

*Richard Hall, former England Under-21 captain,
over 250 Premiership appearances*

The first question that needs to be answered is: 'Why have a chapter specifically on children and young adults?' When I first joined Ipswich, some coaches and managers treated young players as 'mini adults', giving them exactly the same drills they used in the senior training programmes. These days we know this is not appropriate; we must take care to distinguish our conditioning programmes. This chapter is intended to give you a basic grounding in child physiology and the effects of conditioning on young players, so that you can bear these points in mind when developing conditioning programmes. But it is only a basic overview; I strongly recommend that you seek out further reading (there are many good books) if you are keen to gain a detailed understanding on this subject.

There have been huge developments in sports science in the past ten years and it is now obvious to us that there are glaring physiological differences between full-grown adults, young children and developing young adults. Not only do we have to allow for young players' capabilities to complete drills (which perhaps we always did do), but we also have to consider the impact of each and every conditioning drill on the physical development of that young player (which we certainly did not consider many years ago). Not only could some senior drills not help a young player develop, but they could actually have a negative impact of their development.

Another key issue that we have to bear in mind is that, physically, children develop at different ages. Chronological age is not a perfect marker of physical maturity. I have seen many early developers have an advantage in football because of their size and strength and then, when they stop growing, other players catch up and the early developer loses one of their advantages in being noticed. This has to be taken into account when planning conditioning for young players; not only will you have to differentiate according to position (Chapter 1) and time of season (Chapter 2), but also for a player's physical development. Whoever said coaching young players was the easy option was very wrong.

The facts to back it up

Like every good professional, I have statistics to support my theory that a structured approach to conditioning young players can lead to great improvements. The following are some interesting patterns that have emerged during my time with the Academy players at Ipswich Town.

> 'Work hard, be open to new ideas and techniques, and above all, do it with a smile.'
> *Nicky Forster, former England Under-21 international,*
> *over 500 League appearances*

The youth of today

I have read and spoken to many youth coaches who maintain that due to the marked rise in television viewing hours and increased use of computer games, passive recreation is now the norm for most children and consequently they find it hard to be physically active. Generally I would agree with this observation, and that is why playing football (or any other sport) is so important for children's health and welfare.

However, having worked with the Youth Academy for many years, I have not seen any change in the levels of physical activity among children who are committed to their sports – they have similar levels of physical ability as Academy players did a number of years ago. (This is based on the results of the regular testing we do on players from the ages of 13–19.)

These are elite children and junior players, so you would expect them to be fit, but I am convinced that their levels of physical activity owe as much to their enthusiasm as their talent. Not every child will become an elite player, but if we help them to enjoy their sport then I have no doubt that we can halt this disturbing trend towards obesity and the resulting poor health that we see in our children today.

Fitness makes the difference

Over the years, there has been a clear trend in the profile of Academy players (from 13/14 onwards) who made their debut with the first team at a later age (17 onwards). As a rule, those who make it feature in the top 25% of the majority of conditioning tests. This is an important point to make to any young players that you coach, as they can sometimes be a bit complacent and believe that natural skill and talent will be enough to make it. But the stats are clear – it also requires hard work. Basically, you need to be in the top quarter of aerobic/anaerobic fitness to have a chance to go on and play for the first team!

Let me give you a simple example of this concerning two young players (first-year scholars). The first was probably one of the most gifted players (this was the opinion of many coaches) I have seen in many years, but he would not or could not run. The second player, also talented, did not have half the ability of the first player, but was naturally very fit, wanted to learn, and had that horrible thing called pace! At the beginning, it was thought that both players would make a living from the game. As they went through the ranks (under-16s, under-18s and then reserve team football), the ability and the desire to run became more and more important. The first player's obvious lack of conditioning overshadowed his natural ability when he started to play the adult game, to the point where he was released as a 19-year-old (he became a luxury player in the modern game), while the second player, because of his attitude, good coaching and his immense natural fitness, made his first-team debut as an 18-year-old and played for England as a 22-year-old. I have seen many talented youngsters fall down like this.

Weight training

There has been a great deal written about whether weight training should be endorsed for youths and young adults. In my view, it is acceptable so long as the players are at a suitable level of physical development (see below), have been fully coached in the correct techniques for lifting weights, and undertake a structured weight training programme. This is the approach that we have adopted at the Academy and the results speak for themselves.

The following is based on five years' analysis, with first-year youth/Academy players, with each intake averaging eight new players. In 1994 and 1995, there was no conditioning coach at the club and the players took part in an unstructured weights programme. Each group put on 1.91kg and 2.17kg in weight per player, on average, per year, respectively. The post-conditioning coach years – 1996, 1997 and 1998 – when a structured programme was adopted, the groups put on 3.81kg,

4.03kg and 3.58kg in weight per player, respectively. This analysis suggests a structured weights programme can assist and increase a player's physical development and ensure he reaches his full potential, in terms of strength.

Natural development cannot be changed but it can be helped along. Another example is of a tall, slim-built Irish under-17 international with the potential to become a star of the future. He has been at the club for 20 months and with a good weights and nutrition programme, good attitude, hard work, and natural development, has gone from 64kg to 75kg. There has been no change in body fat, and he has grown 2cm. We have many other similar examples.

Body fat percentages were not available for the first two years of the analysis, but the last three years' body fat levels stayed the same or were slightly reduced. Also, there was no significant difference in height growth between the five different years.

TRAINING MYTH

'No pain, no gain.'

I first heard this quote in the military. There are times you have to work to your maximum to stimulate muscle fibre to get stronger and quicker, but there are other times you can improve fitness, gain strength and improve your aerobic capacity without working to your maximum.

The key to speed

We also conducted a 12-week experiment with 14–15-year-old Academy players to find the quickest way to improve a young player's speed. We used two groups and gave them different programmes. Each group had eight players and all of them completed the experiment.

Group A	Twice a week for 12 weeks undertook barbell work, lunges, squats, dead lifts, snatch, etc. (techniques were pre-taught over several months).
Group B	Twice a week for 12 weeks undertook body movements, awareness, technique and agility speed work (this group had also done pre-taught barbell technique work over several months).

The groups were tested using the T-agility speed test (see page 67) before the programme and again after completion. Here are the final results:

Group A	five out of eight got quicker by 1–3%
Group B	All eight got quicker by 2–4%

The conclusion is clear – the quickest way to develop speed initially, is by using body movement and agility work. I have no doubt that weight training does improve speed, but it is a long-term process which has to be done at the right time and right age. For me, the priority for young players (and adult players if they have not been taught) is body movement, awareness, technique, etc., because we are trying to 'awaken' what is already there. It is a more natural way to develop speed. It may be short-term, but it works.

Key age groups

When developing conditioning programmes for children and young players, I typically use three groups:

Pre-growth spurt (boys)	9–13/14 yrs
Post-growth spurt (boys)	13/14–16 yrs
Academy players	16–19 yrs

Remember the point made at the beginning of the chapter, that children develop at different ages. It is not enough to say that all boys will have finished their main growth spurt by the age of 14. Nor can you say that boys and girls will develop at the same age – they do not. The exercises below are intended to aid your planning; they are not a shortcut to avoid the hard work of developing programmes for individuals.

Pre-growth spurt

At this age, the emphasis should be on fun – let the children just get on with the game. All the aerobic and anaerobic work that they need to develop will be achieved just by playing football. Conditioning training will also be limited by time, as young children should not exercise for prolonged periods. As this is the case, ball work is often the priority.

Adapted light strength exercises – with technique and posture high on the list of priorities – should be encouraged, as should working on developing proprioception – the body's natural balance reflexes – and core stability work, although they may find this difficult to understand. It is very much about education at this early age – setting in place good habits that young players will take with them for the rest of their lives. Some of the exercises may not help a great deal now (although they certainly won't do any harm) but they condition the player's mind to do them as a matter of routine later on when they will help conditioning.

Examples of exercises they should be doing include:

- Box/knee press-ups.
- Adapted star jumps.
- Simple burphes (a squat thrust followed by a standing vertical jump).

- Dorsi raisers.
- Adapted sit-ups

SAQ (speed, agility and quickness) development and sprint drills are also good at this age, as long as the sessions are short and the emphasis is on technique with plenty of rest between efforts. Dynamic stretching routines can also be adopted during these sessions.

At this early stage it is also possible to include some adapted first-team routines/drills, such as body movement and awareness (speed) drills. Children often enjoy these drills and it is good for them to feel that they are training just like the 'grown-up' players.

TRAINING BRIEF - MATCH PREPARATION

Physical preparation for the game not only includes conditioning but also refuelling, tactics and mental preparation. Players should ensure they are totally refuelled and hydrated from their last game (especially if it was only a few days earlier) or training session. Our analysis shows that having a Thursday off (before a Saturday game) instead of the normal Wednesday off improves the physical performance of the team on Saturday (tapering). However, this should only be followed if physical performance is the priority, in other words, if mental or tactical issues are the priority, it will probably be better to have the Wednesday off.

One other major factor that should also be considered during preparation is when and how you travel to away games, as long-distance travel can affect the physical performance of a team.

Post-growth spurt

Again, the educational element is important with this group. By now they should have developed sound training habits, so you can move on to laying down foundations for the principles of conditioning. This is the age to introduce conditioning and techniques as its own components; for example, aerobic and anaerobic sessions, strength work using static machines, free weights and medicine balls, more advanced core stability, SAQ development and continuation of speed work. You can also introduce resistance speed work, i.e. Frappier, bungee, etc.

Players can also continue to work on adapted first-team conditioning drills, such as speed relay races and bleep tests, etc. Not only does this help motivate the players but it also prepares those who will go on to train at senior level.

USING THE DRILLS IN THE BOOK

Chapter 5 contains the key conditioning drills that I have developed over the years. If you intend to use these with young players, be sure to note which drills are suitable. The information panel clearly highlights which drills can be used by pre-adolescent and post-adolescent/adult players. Drills which can be used for young players will have information on how they can be adapted.

Academy players

This can be an interesting period for the conditioning coach, as some physically advanced players may be involved with the first team in the professional game or playing with adults in the amateur game. If you take an Academy player as an example, this is a period of immense change, especially in the first six months after turning 16. Their lifestyle will completely change, going from six to seven hours of relatively sedentary activity at school to an environment of three to four hours a day of physical activity. It is not that much different for the amateur players – the transition from school to full-time work can be pretty demanding, physically. This is a vulnerable period, so avoid too much too soon.

In the professional game there tends to be many niggling injuries in the first few months. Conditioning has to be a long-term plan of two years or more, and this is especially true in relation to strength work.

This group of players can do the majority of the conditioning and testing that adults do, with only minor adaptations (such as more rest and regeneration); it just needs some common sense – remember that these young men may still be growing.

What you need to know as a coach – the effects of conditioning

As I said earlier, there are many books and resources dedicated to physiology and the effects of training on a child's physical development. This is a specialist subject and I cannot hope to cover it in depth in this chapter. Rather, the following is intended to give you an overview of the key points that you should bear in mind.

Anatomy

- Ossification (hardening of bones by the laying down of calcium) is not complete until 18–20 years old and in some adults as late as 25.
- Bone growth is dramatically affected by the growth spurt (generally this occurs in girls at 10–12 and boys at 12–14). This may cause a decrease in co-ordination, and make the player susceptible to injury, lack of enthusiasm and a loss of form.

- Basic body types: endomorph (plump) and mesomorph (muscular) stop growing earlier, therefore other children catch up. The third body type is ectomorph (lean and slim).

Physiological differences between adults and children
- Children have smaller hearts and lungs in proportion to their body size.
- The surface area of the lungs is less so the rate of diffusion of gases is lower.
- Children have a lower stroke volume (amount of blood pumped per beat).
- Children have a higher heart rate at rest and during exercise.
- Children breathe faster than adults.

Note: it is inappropriate to use heart rates for a set age with children as there can be huge differences in body size, muscle mass and heart volume when children are the same age.

Children's anaerobic system
This does not develop until after puberty for several reasons, mainly connected with energy forms – ATP (adonine triphosphate), glycogen, creatin phosphate and lactic acid – which are used in developing the body during puberty, and whose natural course should not be interrupted. Therefore, before puberty, children who can run are simply good runners with no real preference for distance. However, after puberty, the balance changes and they become more specialist as their dominant muscle type develops, i.e. fast twitch (broadly speaking, good for short explosive sprints) and slow twitch (good for endurance). It is interesting to note that while training has some effect on the balance of fast twitch/slow twitch muscle, it seems that the biggest factor is genetic.

Add to this the fact that younger children have a lower concentration level and appear to work best in short periods of activity, it can be seen that interval training is the best form of exercise for the pre-pubescent child. It will enhance motivation, attention and allow adequate rest periods, prevent overheating and dehydration. It will also avoid any adverse effects on their physical development.

Temperature control and fluid loss
Children rely much more on radiation and convection to dissipate heat from the skin (rather than sweating; the little sweating that they do is likely to be from the head and not the body). The sweating process only becomes fully functional around puberty. Children have higher skin temperatures than adults and the cooling process of sweating is started at a higher core temperature:

9–10-year-olds sweat 350ml per sq metre of skin.

12–13-year-olds sweat 400–500ml per sq metre of skin.

Adults sweat 600–800ml per sq metre of skin.

In cold environments children are more vulnerable to hypothermia than adults (due to their lower body fat levels). Due to their high breathing rate and less body fluid it is easy for children to become dehydrated in warm conditions. Give children a break every 20 minutes in warm conditions for them to rehydrate.

'When I was a player in the eighties, there were no real conditioning programmes. As my playing days progressed, programmes were being introduced which, on reflection, could have made me a better player had I begun them in my earlier career.'

Tony Humes, coach, over 400 League appearances

Flexibility

This is often defined as the range of movement around the joint or series of joints. We start to lose flexibility at a very early age, maybe as early as seven years old for boys. It is often a forgotten component of conditioning.

Preventative measures to avoid growth-related injuries

- Avoid excessive training loads (especially during the growth spurts).
- Be aware there can be up to a four-year developmental difference within the same age group.
- Encourage children to stretch at an early age.
- Avoid too much high-impact work.

Skills development and learning styles

- Children's neuro-muscular systems are not fully developed, so co-ordination can be difficult. To stimulate development introduce SAQ and similar drills.
- Their reaction time is slower.
- Memory and concentration skills are not fully developed; children lose concentration quickly (for psychological reasons and through boredom).
- It is important we develop simple ball, rugby, balloon or bean bag games to help develop co-ordination and balance. Recently I was listening to a interview with the late George Best, and the interviewer asked what he thought made him a great player. He replied that apart from the obvious, speed, etc . . . it was his balance.

Setting a conditioning programme for young players

Essentially, so long as you remember that children develop at different ages, there is no difference between developing a programme for young players or an adult team. Simply follow the guidance in Chapter 2. However, there are a couple of things to bear in mind: be sure that the players are ready to take part in conditioning training (by asking the questions below) and be clear as to the reasons why you have developed a conditioning programme for young players.

Questions to be asked before introducing a conditioning training programme

Before you put any young player or team on a conditioning programme, ask yourself the following questions. If the answer to any of them is 'no' then you need to plan some more and rethink your approach.

- Is the child/juvenile ready to participate physically in a conditioning programme?
- Is the child/juvenile ready to participate psychologically and emotionally?
- Is the conditioning programme suitable?
- Does the coach/conditioner understand the correct techniques and safety issues?
- Is the programme planned with a long-term goal?
- Have you made sure that you are aware of any relevant physical injury history?

Benefits of a conditioning programme

Before you develop a conditioning programme, you must be clear what it, and each of its component elements, is intended to achieve. The following list should help give you some focus.

- To improve muscular strength and endurance.
- To provide a positive influence on the body's composition.
- To improve strength and balance around the joints.
- To improve techniques and postures, core stability.
- To promote cardio-vascular performance.
- To promote a physical self-esteem and body image (confidence in your physical appearance).
- To reduce sporting injuries.
- To provide a positive influence on other sporting performance.
- To educate the importance of conditioning in football.
- To improve/maintain flexibility.
- To improve quality of lifestyle.

Testing young players

As with adults, it is worth testing youth players to monitor their progress and to ensure that the conditioning programme is having the desired affect. At the Academy, testing children does not start until after the growth spurt. (We do test younger children, but only to confirm if the programmes are working or not. They do not see the results.) Before this age, we limit the number of conditioning drills and do not wish to put unnecessary pressure on the children by testing them; as I have said, fun is the key for younger players.

We use three basic tests for the Academy at Ipswich Town:

- T-agility speed test (see Chapter 4).

- Bleep test.

- Strength test (upper body).

The tests vary according to the time of the year (and season) and the player's training schedule. Also, as the player gets older and develops (typically 16+) the variety of tests increases.

With the T-agility speed test and bleep test there are no adaptations from first-team testing; it is the same test. The strength test differs between age groups and the test contents are subject to available equipment, if any, and what you believe you should be testing. For me, there are no set standards. To give an example, the first-team strength test includes dumbbells and barbells, medicine balls (10kg and 9kg), chin-up bar and inclined press-up. The 15-year-old test includes several static strength machines. The strength test is a home-made, safe test which is dependent on the equipment available.

TRAINING MYTH

'If you exercise long and hard enough, you will always get the results you want.'

In reality, genetics plays an important role in how people respond to exercise. Your development of strength, speed and endurance may be different from that of other people you know; we are all individuals and eventually will reach our limit.

Multi-stage fitness test – the bleep test

This test (an aerobic, tape-based, shuttle test) is designed to test aerobic fitness. It is based on a series of shuttle runs over a fixed distance timed to an audible 'bleep' which gradually increases in frequency so that the player being tested speeds up their runs the further into the test they get. The player will end up with a score according to how long they were able to keep up with the timing of the bleep.

The following test results are from Academy players and can act as benchmark data.

	Under-16			Under-15		Under-14	
	mid-season	early-season	previous season	mid-season	early-season	mid-season	early-season
Player A	13.6	-	12.0	12.6	12.3	12.7	12.5
Player B	13.2	11.9	12.0	11.1	11.5	11.6	11.5
Player C	13.0	12.5	12.2	11.9	11.4	11.7	11.4
Player D	13.0	13.3	12.7	11.2	-	11.9	11.8
Player E	12.9	-	11.9	12.7	12.2	11.3	11.9
Player F	12.9	12.5	12.3	11.7	11.3	11.1	10.4
Player G	12.6	13.2	12.5	11.4	11.0	10.1	10.8
Player H	12.3	12.0	11.6	11.4	-	10.3	10.2
Player I	11.9	11.5	11.5	10.9	-	10.3	-
Player J	11.6	11.4	-	-	-	10.0	9.9
Player K	11.4	11.3	11.0	-	-	-	-
Player L	11.3	10.6	10.2	-	-	-	-

T-agility speed test

See page 67 for full details on setting up this test.

Again, the following results, based on the average of three runs, are from Academy players and can be used as benchmark data.

	Under-16		Under-15		Under-14
	mid-season	early-season	mid-season	early-season	early-season
Player A	9.25	9.17	9.58	9.43	10.00
Player B	9.28	9.39	-	9.52	10.00
Player C	-	9.45	9.56	9.66	10.33
Player D	-	9.46	-	9.68	10.10
Player E	9.95	9.46	9.81	9.72	10.16
Player F	9.35	9.47	9.55	9.77	10.17
Player G	-	9.48	9.71	9.83	10.25
Player H	9.74	9.56	-	10.00	10.28
Player I	10.10	9.84	10.00	10.03	10.28
Player J	-	9.98	10.00	10.05	10.29
Player K	9.31	10.00	10.05	10.18	10.37
Player L	9.25	-	9.84	10.18	10.37
Player M	9.33	-	-	10.25	-

Strength test

As already stated, the strength test should be designed depending on the equipment available. Therefore, there are no standard results. However, in its most basic form, let us use the full press-up as a simple guide.

- 13–14-year-olds. The average for this age group is between 35–60.
- 15–16-year-olds. The average for this age group is between 45–70.
- 17–19-year-olds. The average for this age group is between 50–105.

These numbers are based on working to exhaustion failure, i.e. 'until you drop'!

4 SPEED

This chapter will look at one specific component of conditioning – speed. It will look at why it is so important and how it can be developed in every player.

This chapter will cover:
- The importance of speed in the modern game at every level.
- A brief overview of the sports science behind sprinting.
- The stages of sprinting.
- The development of speed and speed training.
- Speed testing.

Speed – The Competitive Edge

In the previous chapters, I have emphasised that there are a number of components to fitness and that it is the conditioning coach's responsibility to develop a programme which looks at every element. So why do I then devote a chapter to just one component? The simple reason is that in the modern game, speed is the most valuable commodity – it has become the competitive edge.

When managers and coaches discuss a player's physical attributes the two phrases I always hear are, 'The boy has got three lungs' and 'How quick is *he*?!' Whether talking about our team or the opposition, pre- or post-match, I must hear those remarks at least two dozen times a season! I was recently talking to a young, up-and-coming coach in a top league, and he told me how they had spotted a young soccer player during a pre-season game (against non-league opponents) whose pace was frightening. After doing some research, they signed him and he had gone on to score goals for his professional league club and also represent his country at full international level.

It is worth stating again. Speed is *the* competitive edge, especially in football. I have worked with players who may not have been the most skilful, tactically aware or aerobically fit, but they have one thing in common – the ability to accelerate, maintain, endure and change direction at high speed better than most other players on the pitch or training field. All these players have made a good living from the game. I have also noticed over the last three years (thanks to Prozone) that seven out of the nine teams that were promoted to the Premiership had five or more players with tremendous pace (9.1m/s+ on a regular basis), which is above average for the league.

Every player (especially younger and Academy players) has the potential to improve their speed. Although speed is a natural component of a player's make-up, to a large extent you can improve a player's speed by a significant amount if the programme is well structured and the player works hard with the right attitude. Experience has shown me that players who are sceptical or are 'non-believers' tend to improve less than players with open minds.

You can improve every player's speed whether they are natural or not. To what extent is the difficult question!

TRAINING BRIEF – RECOVERY AND COOL-DOWN

This should be an integral part of any training programme. Recovery is the phase during which the body adapts and recovers from training or a match. There are important physiological benefits to be gained by cooling down after a very hard game or training session. Correct cool-downs promote the removal of waste products such as lactic acid from the body. Ideally, a 10–12-minute session at low intensity, including stretching, should suffice. Eating within an hour or two after a game or a hard training session (the most beneficial window of opportunity for re-fuelling) is highly recommended.

Sleep is also an underestimated aid to recovery. During sleep rejuvenation and repair occurs, especially to areas where the blood supply is poor (ligaments, tendons, etc.). Try not to disturb sleep patterns. Short naps during the day can be useful in promoting recovery. Passive methods to promote recovery include massages, pools, jacuzzis and ice baths, if used correctly and at the appropriate time.

However, in reality, it can sometimes be difficult to implement some of the above, especially cool-downs after training sessions.

The theory

There is a fairly simple process that leads to a player moving: the player decides to run (mental), this message is transmitted to the muscles (via the nervous system), the muscles engage and the player moves.

There has been a great deal of research into this process and current sports science is beginning to blur the distinctions between these stages. For example, there is evidence to suggest that, through conditioning, muscles can develop the capacity to 'think', thus reacting almost before they have received the message to engage from the brain.

However, the basic principles remain. By understanding these principles you can incorporate activities into day-to-day training. For example, set a word of the day at the beginning of every session that, when heard, the players have to react to in a certain way, such as sitting on the ground or sprinting to a cone or a particular coach. At a random point during the session, particularly between drills when players are mentally switched off, call out the word. The last person to react has to do a forfeit. Not only does this keep the players mentally alert but it gets them used to reacting without thinking, which could save that all important 1/100th of a second.

Again, the science of speed is an area where I urge you to do your own research – there is a wealth of information out there to look at.

Fast twitch/slow twitch muscles

One area that has received a great deal of attention in recent years is the difference between fast twitch and slow twitch muscle fibres, and it is worth a quick mention to clarify.

Fast twitch – called or classified as type IIa and IIb.
Slow twitch – called or classified as type I.

- Fast twitch muscle fibres make you move quickly and explosively.
- Slow twitch muscle fibres are required for endurance and stability in any movement.

In this chapter we are interested in the fast twitch – speed.
- Fast twitch, type IIa, can be defined with speed endurance.
- Fast twitch, type IIb, can be defined with two or three sprints.

As a game comes to an end and players tire or their sprints are longer we tend to tap in more to type IIa.

Finally and most importantly for us, there is a third type of fast twitch muscle fibre, type IIc, what I call free radicals or floaters. This can be trained either to fast or slow with good training programmes and lifestyle.

The stages of sprinting

Coaches are correct in believing that speed includes acceleration, maximum speed phase and deceleration phase (when you can no longer maintain your top speed). However, there are other components to be aware of to improve speed.

There are seven physical and mental stages of an average sprint:
1. Mental brightness, alertness and awareness (speed of thought).
2. Anticipation and/or reaction.
3. Golden step (first movement, positive).

4. Upper body awareness/movement.

5. Initial steps (acceleration phase).

6. Technique/running mechanics.

7. Deceleration (point you cannot maintain top speed).

I have learned that if you can improve two or more of these components (either physical or mental), statistically you will be faster.

Speed of thought

Mental brightness, awareness, alertness, call it what you will, this is the first stage of the process and, thus, the key. How many times have you watched a game on TV and heard the commentator lament of a player, 'He switched off for a minute'? You will hear it all the time.

It is also a psychological demand and so one that is often overlooked on the training ground. There are three elements to mental brightness: concentration, research and the ability to learn on the pitch. The first is vital, a player must develop the ability to focus and pay attention to the game from the first whistle to the last. It sounds easy, but as anyone who has driven for long periods will know, concentration is a tiring business.

The player should also do his homework, where possible, on the team he is playing and the player he is likely to come up against. What are their strengths and weaknesses? Are they slow to recover from sprints? Are they a short team which struggles with the long ball? Do they launch most of their attacks down the left? Then, with individuals, are they left- or right-footed? Do they have a particular trick they like to use? What is the best way for the player to deal with all these variables?

Then there is the information to process on the day. Does the opponent marking the player have a niggling injury, is the wind holding the ball up, what's the surface like?

Every single one of these factors must be considered and processed before a player starts his sprint. And they say football is not a thinking person's game!

'Be prepared to pay the price for success. Does physical strength lead to mental toughness or mental toughness lead to physical strength?'

Bryan Klug, Ipswich Town assistant manager,
former England Under-17 international

Anticipation and reaction

Speed work in football should be about anticipation: 'Where is my team-mate going to put the ball?' or 'The opposition is not going to get that ball, can I get to it?' This is the second mental stage and involves processing all the information received in the first stage and coming to a conclusion.

This mental phase makes all the difference and is the root of the phrase: 'You don't need to be fast to be quick'. I have worked with several players who, when doing speed testing, have not had particularly good test results, but watching them play and train on numerous occasions they seem to always get to the ball first, intercept the ball or score goals when their 'marker' is much faster than they are. The ability to be one step ahead of your opponent psychologically, to have a 'footballing brain' or to have superior reactions, will make the difference at any level.

The golden step

This is the first physical stage of the sprint process. The 'golden step' is an American term which basically means that the first step should being a positive movement, i.e. from a standing start – a forward wide step (not a backwards step), etc. It begins motion and starts to transfer body weight in the right direction.

Upper body awareness

This is often an underestimated element of sprint work; many people consider the arms to be the only significant part of the upper body when it comes to running. The upper body should be like a pendulum, working in synchronisation with the legs. When you start a sprint, try to throw your upper body vigorously forwards (in the direction of first step). If you do not react and work your legs quickly, you end up flat on your face. When turning, throw your upper body (in a controlled fashion) into the direction you are going. Your legs will follow. Use your body weight to assist you and take some of the load of your legs.

Acceleration phase

One of the key things that you need to do as a conditioning coach is to learn lessons from every sport; here is a prime example. Watch athletics and see how short-distance sprinters come out of the blocks. Look at their initial steps and body movement; how they keep low, take wide steps and sway their body to give them the power and acceleration to start a sprint. Even in football with walking or rolling starts, we can learn from these starts.

Technique and running mechanics

I'll just give a brief overview of the key components:

- Stride frequency (foot-to-ground contact). Known as stride rate, leg speed or leg cycles – measured in steps per second.
- Stride length. The ideal stride length is an important part of reaching your potential. Understriding or overstriding will affect your speed.
- Running economy. Basically this means how everything works together and which part of the body must be relaxed while sprinting and not wasting unnecessary energy (i.e. hands, head and upper body).
- Body movement (arms, etc.). Not only the use of arms working or pumping from the shoulder, but using your whole upper body to help you change direction etc. Lead with the upper body
- Knee lift. Generally speaking, your knee lift is the amount of force generated when your foot hits the ground, the least possible time your foot stays on the floor and what I call the butt kick (foot-to-buttocks).

One thing to consider with running technique is that, generally, the younger the player (especially children), the more influence you will have on them. You will find it difficult to influence the styles of players in their twenties. Time might be better spent on other stages of the sprint process.

Deceleration phase

Speed endurance training will increase the duration that maximum speed can be maintained. Players should also be encouraged to decelerate in a controlled way; not only will this reduce the chance of injury, but it means that the player is poised and balanced, ready to react to the situation.

Development of speed

For me, the physical side of the development of speed is split into two main areas:
1. Good core and strength base (foundation).
2. Field work – speed drills and techniques.

'Set yourself targets - when you reach your target, set a higher target, and keep striving to better yourself this way.'

Matt Holland, former Republic of Ireland international, over 450 Premiership and League appearances

Core and strength base

This foundation training can be included during part of the close season and pre- and early-season cycles. It will then be phased out as the season progresses and the players get all the speed work they need from playing games.

Once again there are many good books out there that will cover these areas and exercises. Exercises to consider including include:

- Core stability. This is the foundation of any strength work. Concentrates on the muscles around the stomach and lower back, may include buttocks, quads and hamstring.
- Upper body strength work. This area should target the shoulders, arms, chest, stomach and back.
- Lunges. A good all-round exercise to develop the quads, hamstring and buttocks.
- Squats. As above, an exercise to develop the quads, hamstring, buttocks and calves.
- Frappier system. Develops speed and power by using a treadmill on an incline in short bursts; see page 109.
- Step-ups. Another good exercise to develop the leg muscles.
- Bungees. A dynamic form of exercise to overload all the muscles used while sprinting; see page 127.
- Plyometrics. Highly explosive exercises that enable a muscle to reach maximal strength in a short period of time.
- Medicine ball work. Dynamic all-round work; see page 141.

Field work

This work can be undertaken during the early phases (especially when the core and strength work are done) of the season. The intention is to build on the foundation work developed earlier in the season, using drills to hone technique.

Typical drills include the following:

- Foot-to-ground contact drills.
- SAQ drills.
- Body movement.
- Acceleration and techniques.

When working on these drills you must ensure that the players are working to their maximum, otherwise they will struggle to see the benefits of this training.

Soccer is a multi-directional, multi-paced, explosive, but aerobically-based game; therefore drills should simulate what happens in a game. Note that many sprints only last two to four seconds with the maximum sprints usually 70 metres. These are drills that are done on a pitch.

Dos and don'ts of speed training

Do:
- Train early in a session (after warm-up).
- Use your imagination (relays, rugby ball, etc.).
- Majority of sprints between two and five seconds.
- Train multi-directional sprints.
- Short sessions – 1:6 or 1:8 ratio effort to rest.
- Speed work with or without a ball.
- Make sprints competitive.
- Ensure players' attitude is right.

Don't
- Train without strength base.
- Exceed more than 60–70m in sprint work.
- Work every day, three to four sessions a week, depending on games.
- Do speed work when players are tired.
- Work less than 100%.

Reversibility
It is important to mention reversibility with speed. Analysis shows that players lose pace very quickly if they don't use it. We have numerous examples of this, from the obvious one of players being injured, to the not-so-obvious of players not pushing themselves in training, being lazy, and losing over half a metre over a ten-metre sprint. Use it or lose it.

Speed tests
One of the most important reasons for testing speed is to show the players their progress and to prove they are getting quicker. Once you have done this, you are halfway there.

There is a whole range of speed tests that you can use, or you can make up your own. I have found that the following work best for me.

The T-agility test

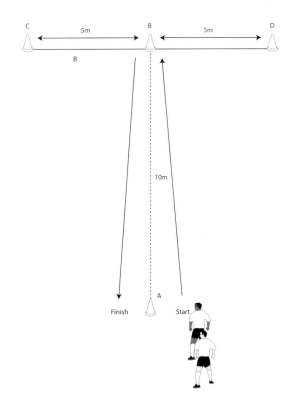

The T-agility test is great for testing players' short sprint and change of direction capabilities. This test is best undertaken during the early- to mid-season. The results should be based on the average of three runs.

To set up the test, you will need four cones and a stopwatch.

The test:
- The player starts at A; start the stopwatch on the first limb movement.
- He sprints to B, then makes a 90° turn around the cone and heads for C.
- From C, the player makes a 180° turn around the cone and heads for D.
- He then takes a 180° turn at D, before making his way back to B and a further 90° turn and then back, past the start (A).

As a rough indication:
- Under 9.10 seconds is excellent.
- Under 9.70 seconds is average.
- Over 9.70 seconds is poor.

The 40-metre straight line sprint test

This test measures straight line speed (usually the longest sprint players will do in a game). The reason I use this test is because the distance is easily accessible. Most full-size pitches have 39–39.5 metres already marked out – the width of the penalty box.

The test is simple. The player starts at one end of the penalty box. As soon as you see his first leg movement, start the stopwatch. The sprint ends when the player crosses the line at the opposite end of the penalty box.

Take the average of three runs, with approximately two to four minutes rest between each run.

Any time under 4.75 seconds is outstanding.

Any time under 5 seconds is very good.

Any time over 6.5 seconds is slow.

> **TRAINING MYTH**
>
> 'Test results never lie.'
>
> Although test results are the best way to monitor the players' physical state, they can be misleading, for example, if the players' attitude towards them is poor or if they are complacent. Results can also be affected if the tests are done at the wrong time or if the variables, such as time of year, are not taken into account.

Jump test

This test, which measures maximal strength in as short a time as possible, i.e. power, can be undertaken at any time of the season.

Ideally, this test should use an electronic jump mat, although it is possible to use the old method of jumping against a wall, marking the maximum height of the player's jump with chalk and then subtracting their full reach height from the total distance to give you the jump height. The result is the average of three jumps.

The test:
- The player starts from a standing position.
- He then bends his knees (impulse) before performing maximal contraction of the leg extensors to achieve maximal height.

Here are some examples of results from players taken at the beginning of the season (August):

17-year-old centre back	43cm	17-year-old centre forward	48cm
First-team centre back	55cm	First-team full back – junior	50cm
First-team centre back	45cm	First-team centre forward	56cm
First-team full back – senior	45cm	First-team midfielder	46cm
Internal centre forward	58cm	Goalkeeper – senior	62cm
First-team midfielder	48cm	17-year-old centre forward	46cm

Sprint test

This test is used to measure flat-out speed. It is best used early in the season and requires the use of some pretty technical equipment – electronic gates – although it may be possible to replicate with cones and stopwatches if there is a timekeeper at each gate who is accurate with the stopwatch.

This test requires a start line and gates set at 5m, 10m and 20m.

The test is run with two versions – standing sprint and rolling sprint. For the standing sprint, the player starts on the start line; a 2m run-up is allowed for the rolling sprint.

Examples Only	Standing Sprint			Rolling Sprint		
	5m	10m	20m	5m	10m	20m
18-year-old centre forward	1.07	1.77	3.01	0.85	1.38	2.76
First-team centre forward	1.09	1.80	3.10	0.85	1.40	2.73
Senior centre back	1.11	1.83	3.29	0.91	1.43	3.02
First-team midfielder	1.09	1.77	3.29	0.85	1.38	2.91
17-year-old midfielder	1.34	2.09	3.42	0.87	1.56	2.87
Released Academy midfielder	1.59	1.85	3.28	0.94	1.52	2.76
Released Academy midfielder	1.16	1.92	3.33	0.92	1.66	3.04
Senior first-team full back	1.01	1.67	3.28	0.87	1.30	2.86
First-team midfielder – wide	1.14	1.89	3.02	0.82	1.47	2.80
Released reserve midfielder	1.04	1.70	3.31	0.88	1.33	2.96
Academy goalkeeper	1.17	1.96	3.29	0.87	1.57	2.88
MEAN AVERAGE	1.10	1.81	3.22	0.86	1.41	2.91

Summary sheets

There are a number of ways the results for all of the above tests can be displayed. One summary sheet that I find particularly effective, and which is very popular with both players and coaches, uses colour-coded boxes. These are very easy on the eye.

The following example is for the results from the three tests.

	Jump	Sprint	Agility
Academy centre back			
Senior first-team centre forward			
Senior holding midfielder			
Junior centre forward			
16-year-old centre forward			
Senior first-team full back			
First-team centre back			
First-team squad midfielder			
First-team midfielder			
First-team centre back			
First-team squad midfielder			
Released midfielder			
First-team full back			
First-team centre back			
Academy centre forward			
Academy midfielder			
First-team centre forward			
First-team midfielder			

Key	
Excellent	
Above average	
Average	
Below average	
Poor	

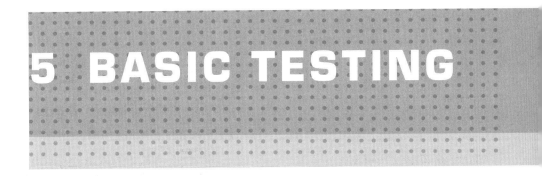

5 BASIC TESTING

This chapter looks at how and why we should test players throughout the season. Any team, whether professionals, amateurs or children, can do the majority of these tests, which are simple and require a minimum of equipment and effort. I have also included a couple of laboratory tests, which may be useful for the amateur clubs who have access to university or college facilities.

This chapter will cover:
- Testing amateur players and children.
- The importance of testing.
- Field tests.
- Laboratory tests.

Amateur testing

When considering testing for amateur teams, the same questions come up as when planning the conditioning programme (see chapter 2): how much time does the team have to train and why does the team play? Generally, the same guidelines apply. If you play for fun and the social side of the game, than testing may not be relevant. If you are a more serious player or are higher up the non-league ladder than testing becomes more relevant and appropriate.

Subject to what standard you play at and how serious you take your soccer, you are looking at between 10%–20% difference between professionals and amateurs. But past testing history will give you a better indication of performance and the effects of the conditioning programme.

Children's testing

For children, I believe testing is only appropriate after growth spurt (see chapter 3 for more information and some sample tests). Some testing might be required to see if specific training programmes are succeeding in their goals and aims. (Results are not given to the children.) Subject to age, the difference between professionals and academy children tends to be between 10%–30%. The difference between academy and the average Saturday and Sunday child is difficult to say, but I do believe there to be a difference, if only because academy children train and play up to three times a week to a moderate to high intensity level out of school hours.

The importance of testing

Testing is vital for a wide range of reasons including the following:
- Assess fitness levels.
- To set programmes and schedules.
- To study the effect of training programmes and matches.
- To turn weaknesses into strengths (team and individual).
- To motivate players and give objective feedback.
- To educate players.
- To assess rehabilitation work and post-injury condition.
- To create future standards and database.
- To monitor overtraining and long rest periods.
- To advise manager of any conditioning issues.

All of these reasons are valid, but before you begin testing your players you must be clear what the purpose is for those tests – which of these reasons are specific to your club?

Remember that 'a test is only as relevant (accurate) as the player's attitude towards it'. I have heard this statement many times, therefore it is of great importance that you ensure testing is a positive experience for the player. In my many years working with players, It is interesting to note, in the professional game and academy level, that players who moan about testing or have a poor attitude towards it tend to be the players who have got something to hide!

The best way to get the players involved and interested in testing is to educate them on the benefits. If you can, use examples from your past experience or use one of the established players at the club as an example (with their permission) – this also has the benefit of winning players over, as many of the junior players in the squad will look up to the established players.

For example, I once worked with a senior player who was still playing the professional game at the highest level at the age of 36. He had a good attitude towards training and had understood the importance of testing to assess his conditioning levels throughout his 20-year career, to the point where even at that age he was still doing 14+ on the bleep test! Another example is of an academy under-15 player of tremendous ability. So skilful was he that coaches' eyes would light up at the mention of his name, though when it came to his fitness there were real concerns. He could barely get around the pitch and used to come last in the bleep test. But through his amazing dedication and will to succeed, he went from a 10.2 to a 14.2 bleep test in just ten months and has now signed a two-year scholarship. (See page 75 for details of the bleep test.)

When to test

Choose the right time to do your testing, Avoid testing players when they are tired or during a hectic schedule of games, for example in the busy Christmas or Easter periods. You might want to think about whether it is realistic or beneficial to test the players right at the end of the season! See chapter 2 for further guidance.

What type of testing

The tests should be as relevant to football as possible. There are dozens of tests/monitoring systems being used in football and opinions differ as to which to use. Facilities, time and budget are big factors to consider when choosing a test. Whatever tests you decide to do, try not to change them, as previous results can tell you a lot when compared to current results.

At Ipswich Town Football Club we use a handful of basic field tests for our first team (backed-up currently by Prozone), reserves, youths and academy players (13–16 year olds). I will show you some of the results which you should try to use as a benchmark to motivate your players. Remember, when testing players it actually becomes a conditioning session within itself.

Keeping test results

Be sure that you have an effective system for recording all your test results – the main benefit of testing comes not from comparing one result against a benchmark figure, but in seeing patterns emerge in a single player's performance over time.

The type of system that you use is purely a matter of personal preference – it could be as simple as a notebook. However, I prefer to store results on a computer using a spreadsheet – this allows me to use the data in a vast number of ways, profiling individual players and comparing players during the season and over the years. It is also very easy to produce graphs and colourful charts which I have found are a particularly effective way of explaining the results to both players and managers.

HEART RATE MONITORS

If you have access to heart rate monitors you should use them during testing. Monitors have many functions but, for me, one of their best features is that they don't lie! If you know a player's maximum heart rate, you will then be able to determine what percentage of their maximum they are working during the tests, which in turn gives you their effort level. There really is nowhere to hide when wearing a monitor.

There are a number of ways to calculate a player's maximum heart rate, the simplest being 220 – age (e.g. a 23-year-old's maximum heart rate will be 220 – 23 = 197). This is an approximate figure and individuals will differ, but it will suit all but the most serious of athletes.

The next stage is to calculate the player's maximum *working* heart rate – not to be confused with maximum heart rate. To do this:

1. The player must find their resting heart rate – this is best done by taking a pulse within ten minutes of waking up in the morning, while still laying down. It is also best to take readings over a period of a week and use an average result.
2. Then subtract the player's resting heart rate from their maximum. For example, our 23-year-old player has a resting heat rate of 58, so this gives him a working heart rate of 139.
3. Finally, you take whatever percentage of working heart rate that the player is aiming for (e.g. 75% would be 139 × 0.75 = 104) and add this to the player's resting heart rate (e.g. 104 + 58 = 162). This gives you the target heart rate that they should aim for.

Broadly, there are three training zones (with the heart rate zones for our 23-year-old player):
- *Low intensity* – 60%–75% (141–162bpm)
- *Moderate intensity* – 75%–85% (162–176bpm)
- *High intensity* – 85%–95% (176–190bpm).

Obviously, the harder the level the less time the player will be able to sustain the pace – you would expect a player to be able to jog at an easy level for an hour or more, whereas 95% would only be sustained for a short *period*.

It is also worth noting that heart rate zones and the use of monitors are of little use when working with children and young players, due to physiological differences.

Field tests

Field tests will form the bulk of testing methods at most clubs – even professional clubs. They are simple to set up, don't require specialist equipment and can easily be incorporated into training sessions.

The following tests are my personal favourites. There are also more tests in Chapters 3 (for young players) and 4 (speed specific).

> 'Be responsible – look after yourself. Enjoy what you do, get yourself mentally right and make the most of your chances. And be sure to eat right and have plenty of rest.'
>
> *Hermann Hreidarsson, Iceland international,*
> *over 250 Premiership and League appearances*

Multistage fitness bleep test

This is the same test that we use when testing young players (see chapter 3). It is an aerobic, progressive shuttle run test that measures aerobic capacity and is used by many clubs and sports.

The test is based on a series of shuttle runs over a fixed distance, timed to an audible 'bleep' which gradually increases in frequency so that the player being tested speeds up the further into the test they get. The frequency of the bleep increases as the player moves through the levels of the test – each level lasts approximately one minute and there are up to 21 levels (although I have never seen anyone get near level 21!).

The player will end up with a score according to the level and number of shuttles within that level that they successfully completed before failing to keep up with the bleep (this is the figure recorded below). A player's VO2 Max score (see below) can be determined by referring this result to the Multistage Fitness Test table – this can be found on the internet, along with details on how to set up this test and sound files for the 'bleeps' which can be downloaded. However, I find it just as useful to record the levels and use these for comparison.

As you will see, we use this test on a regular basis to monitor players – partly because it is a reliable indicator and partly because it is easy to set up. Note that for the July results the early test was taken after five days of pre-season training and the end of month test was on the 23rd day of pre-season training – a well planned pre-season really does make a difference, so have another look at chapter 2.

	early-July	end of July	October/November	February
Young Reserve midfielder	15.2	-	13.4	13.4
Young Reserve midfielder/wing back	14.1	-	15.6	14.1
First-team squad centre back	14.4	14.1	-	-
Young Reserve centre back	13.1	-	-	12.6
Senior first-team full back	13.9	13.1	13.0	13.0
First-team centre forward	13.8	14.7	14.8	14.1
Academy centre forward	13.7	13.1	13.2	12.2
First-team centre back	13.0	13.5	12.0	-
First-team centre back	13.3	13.7	-	-
Academy centre back	13.0	-	12.3	-
First-team midfielder	13.4	13.8	-	-
First-team midfielder	-	13.1	13.1	-
Academy midfielder	12.4	-	12.7	12.3
Academy midfielder	12.4	-	12.7	-
First-team full back	-	-	16.0	14.1
Academy full back	12.3	13.0	-	13.1
Academy centre back	13.1	14.0	12.1	-
Out-of-favour midfielder	-	-	10.1	12.6

Let's look at two case studies of the results, which show how the process of conditioning is affected by influences outside a conditioner's remit. The first study is for the two first-team centre backs: the good news was that as pre-season progressed, the players were getting fitter. However, when one player was re-tested four months into the season his conditioning had dropped, although he was playing very well (you can also see this with the other centre backs). Although there are numerous reasons why this could have happened, in my experience it is because a centre back's position is very specific and his effort is dictated by his own centre forwards' running in training and the opposition's in games. Therefore (see chapter 1) centre backs lose a little bit of their aerobic conditioning during the season. This is because they are not being continually and consistently pressured as is the case with the other eight outfield players, whereas during pre-season they are constantly overloaded. The second case study is of the two centre forwards, who had all four tests completed. In very simple terms, the first-teamer was having a great season, had scored 20 goals and was on fire. The youngster, who was not scoring goals, got dropped from his team and was eventually released. Do not underestimate the mental side of the game and how this affects conditioning.

VO2 MAX

If you scratch the surface of any serious research on conditioning, you will soon come across the phrase VO2 Max. Like much jargon, it sounds very impressive but once it has been explained it is pretty straightforward.

VO2 Max is the is the maximum amount of oxygen in millilitres a person can use in one minute per kilogram of body weight. Put simply, the higher a player's VO2 Max score, the better his fitness and his capacity to exercise at high intensity.

As with any element of fitness, there is a range of factors that can influence performance – age, genetics, health at the time of testing. But the important thing is that a player's VO2 Max capacity can be improved through specific drills and exercises. Most notably, aerobic capacity can be improved by training in a zone of 70%–85% of maximum working heart rate for sustained periods of 20 minutes – this is when the use of heart rate monitors becomes vital (see above).

The 'ideal' VO2 Max score varies from sport to sport. In football, you would be looking for scores in the range of 60–65 ml/kg/min, whereas in endurance sports such as cycling (the Tour de France) it is common to see scores over 75ml/kg/min.

Umbro aerobic capacity test

This test of aerobic capacity takes its name from a book called *Umbro Conditioning for Football*, written in conjunction with the Liverpool John Moore University.

This test itself is pretty simple – the player must run as far as possible in exactly 12 minutes. Ideally, this test should be performed on a running track as it's easy to calculate to total distance covered. However, it can be performed by running round a football pitch as long as the dimensions are known.

One thing to bear in mind, though, are the conditions that each test was conducted under and the effect this may have on results – for example, it is easier to run on a track than it is on grass so you would expect more distance to be covered on the track. This is important when comparing results over a period of time.

Once the test is completed, you use the distance covered to help calculate aerobic capacity by using the formula 0.0225×5.5 metres covered - 11.3. So, if a player covers 3,000 metres their aerobic capacity is 56.2 units. Although this is designed as a physical test, I have also found it a great way to test mental toughness – many of the players I have put through this test have told me that the hardest thing is to keep at your limit for the full 12 minutes.

Here is a sample of results from our players for the 2004/5 season. During this season I learned a lot about giving young players too much of a break during the Christmas period! (16–18-year-olds were the only group re-tested in January.) I made an error in giving that group of players too much of a rest. They had three weeks off, with no game in four weeks, and had a stretching and low intensity programme only. As you can see from the results, four out of the five players came back in poor shape. (Other results with the same group, not published, showed 75% of the players returning in poor shape.) One of the coaches questioned what the youngsters had been up to. Since then, we have given the Academy players ten days' rest during the Christmas period, followed by ten days' moderate to high intensity work, and the results have improved dramatically after a three-week break.

	Pre-Season 2004/5	Pre-Season 2003/4	January 2005	2002/3
Young Reserve midfielder	68.3	69.1	63.4	65.5
First-Team centre back	68.3	65.2	-	-
First-Team midfielder	66.6	66.6	-	60.0
Academy midfielder	66.4	61.7	57.9	-
Reserve midfielder	65.6	63.4	59.0	63.0
First-Team centre forward	64.5	-	-	-
Academy full back	63.0	64.3	53.9	-
First-Team midfielder	61.9	64.9	-	66.9
Academy centre forward	61.8	61.7	-	-
First-Team centre forward	69.4	-	-	65.4
First-Team centre back/midfielder	65.5	66.5	-	-
Amateur midfielder (Trial)	58.9	-	-	-
Reserve centre back	61.3	62.2	62.1	-
First-Team full back	61.0	62.2	-	57.1
First-Team centre back	59.6	69.0	-	58.4
First-Year Academy full back	58.5	-	-	-
First-Year Academy forward	58.0	-	-	-
First-Team centre forward	55.6	59.6	-	60.9
Amateur centre back (Trial)	51.6	-	-	-

12-minute treadmill test

This test is similar to the UMBRO test. It is very simple and, as such, is perfect for players to undertake themselves to monitor their own fitness – this is particularly useful if your team only gets together for training once a week and that time is precious (of course, this supposes that you can trust your players!). Many players I have coached like to use this test to keep a track of their own fitness during the close season and in addition to all the testing we do at the club. I'm a big fan, as anything that helps players to take responsibility for their fitness has to be a good thing.

The test requires players to run as far as they can in 12 minutes – it's that simple. The advantage of using the treadmill is that the distance can be measured with complete accuracy and the player can control their speed. When running this test (and in general when using a treadmill) an incline of 1.0% should be set as this replicates the effort that would be encountered running against the wind outdoors.

When I use this test, I expect all players to complete at least two miles in the 12 minutes. The possible exception are centre backs, but in contrast full backs, midfielders and strikers should comfortably cover this distance.

Here are a couple of samples from a recent test:

- A first-team centre back recorded 2.00 miles – I was happy with this result given his position.
- A first-team wide midfielder set a club record 2.39 miles – a brilliant result.
- A reserve-team midfielder recorded 2.10 miles – not great, but fine considering he was returning from injury.
- A reserve-team centre back recorded 1.85 miles – this is a poor result, but the player was a trialist from a non-league club, which goes to show the difference in fitness at these levels.

Stamina/recovery test

This is a test that I devised some years ago and have continued to use since I joined Ipswich Town. It is based on a similar test that I used in the armed forces, so I found it easy to relate to and had plenty of benchmark data from the six years I spent using it.

The players complete two one-mile runs with an active recovery (i.e. jogging or walking) in between. The first mile is run as a squad and must be completed in six minutes and 30 seconds (for professional players). After a rest phase of three minutes, the players must then run the second mile as individuals as fast as possible.

Some sample results are recorded below. As you can see from the results for 2000/1, our training programmes were showing good progress and players had improved from the previous season. It is also interesting to note that this was the season we finished fifth in the Premiership but the results in November (pre-Prozone), although generally better than pre-season in 1999/2000, were disappointing for me as I had expected bigger improvement. Looking back on it, the previous season finished late due to the play-off final and the new season started early, which meant the players only had four and a half weeks off. Perhaps more importantly it was our first year in the Premiership, so the players were buzzing with self-belief and had a great attitude, hence some excellent pre-season results.

	Pre-Season Test 2000/1	Pre-Season Test 1999/2000	November 2000	Other Scores 1997/8, 1998/9
First-team wing back/midfielder	4.45	5.03	5.00	-
First-team centre forward	4.48	5.13	5.07	-
First-team wing back/full back	5.01	5.30	-	5.35
Reserve midfielder	5.07	5.35	5.13	5.46
Reserve centre forward	5.08	5.21	5.20	-
First-team full back	5.09	-	5.13	-
First-team centre back/midfielder	5.11	-	5.35	-
First-team centre forward	5.20	5.35	5.29	-
First-team midfielder	5.32	5.36	5.29	6.10
First-team wing back/full back	5.32	5.37	5.40	6.12
Academy full back	5.35	5.56	-	-
First-team midfielder	5.13	-	-	5.13
First-team midfielder	5.12	-	-	-
First-team midfielder	5.14	5.30	-	5.48
First-team midfielder	5.44	5.27	5.52	5.58
Academy midfielder	4.57	-	-	5.12
Academy centre back	5.29	-	-	-
Academy full back	5.35	-	-	-
Academy centre forward	6.35	-	-	6.15
Academy full back	5.35	5.40	-	-

Laboratory tests

Not every team will be able to enjoy the luxury of laboratory tests as they require specialised equipment and experts to interpret the results. However, with increasing numbers of colleges and universities running courses in sports science it is worth enquiring as to whether they need 'guinea pig' teams – that way the students get to use your results in their projects while your team gets the benefit of technical testing.

VO2 Max laboratory test

This is the most accurate way to determine a players VO2 Max capacity. Unlike the tests outlined above, it does not require the use of tables on formulae to convert scores into VO2 Max capacity – it measures this directly. This is achieved by the player running on a treadmill at controlled speeds while hooked up to a heart rate monitor and breathing through a mask which analyses the composition of the player's breath. It can also require blood samples being taken.

Needless to say, it can be an expensive way of testing, so we tend to use this only in circumstances when we need completely accurate results. For example, the results below are all from players who were returning from mid- to long-term injuries. They are listed in order of highest to lowest scores with specific reasons for testing.

First-team midfielder   69.0
September – routine testing.

First-team full back   65.8
August – coming back from long-term injury.

First-team midfielder   64.5
September – routine testing.

Young centre back   62.7
July – injured the previous season, just
ensuring he could join in with pre-season.

Young centre back   62.5
August – question marks over his attitude.

First-team midfielder   62.1
December – routine testing.

Young centre back   61.7
September – coming back from long-term injury.

First-team centre forward   61.2
December – routine testing.

First-team centre forward   58.8
September – routine testing.

First-team midfielder   58.8
November – coming back from two major operations.

Young full back   57.3
November – doubts about his conditioning levels.

Young centre forward   55.0
August – coming back from a broken ankle.

First-team full back   51.4
September – big concerns with this player's fitness,
hence re-tested in December after a special ten-week
programme, achieving 56.9.

Academy goalkeeper   50.2
January – routine testing.

Academy centre forward   45.1
August – needed to find out if it was either 'can't run'
or 'won't run'!

Wingate Anaerobic Bike Test

The Wingate Anaerobic Bike Test (WANT) is a very popular laboratory-based anaerobic test – largely because it does not require much in the way of specialist equipment. After a warm-up, the player starts pedalling with no resistance. A resistance (calculated according to the player's body weight) is then placed on the wheel for a period of six seconds and the player must continue pedalling 'flat out'. The number of revolutions the player manages is recorded. After the six seconds, the resistance is removed and the player has 30 seconds: recovery. This is repeated ten times and all results recorded.

Like many fitness tests, these initial results can then be used with a range of formulae to calculate more detailed information. However, as I generally use this test to compare the performance of an individual over time there really is no need.

This test is good to monitor the rate of fatigue that a player experiences over a period of time when working the muscles against resistance – i.e. it looks at power as well as aerobic and anaerobic fitness. Two points can be taken from the results:

- The power of the player – i.e. their output in the first three sprints when the muscles are fresh.

- The rate of fatigue of the player – i.e. percentage decline in performance between the first and last sprint.

	Mean work Production Stage 1 - 3	Mean work Production Stage 7 - 10	Percentage decline between first and last sprint (FATIGUE)
First-team centre forward	6.16	5.55	10
Reserve centre back	6.09	5.19	15
First-team full back	5.59	4.60	18
First-team midfielder	5.54	5.05	9
First-team midfielder	5.58	3.85	30
First-team midfielder	4.41	3.80	14
First-team centre forward	4.80	3.90	18

If you look at the past history of the first-team midfielder with a 30% fatigue level, which is way above the normal, you will see why the fatigue levels are so high. He was a very quick player in his mid-thirties who had not played regular soccer for several months, and when he did play it was in a free/floating role. Age had obviously caught up with him, but also his aerobic capacity was low. We tried to improve his aerobic capacity and then install a speed endurance programme – however, he left the club before we could re-test him. The first-team midfielder with a 9% fatigue level had a VO2 Max of 69%, which is exceptional. He had average pace and was a box-to-box player. We knew what we were going to get from him physically for 90 minutes. We tried to develop his pace by breaking the speed components into specific training regimes (see chapter 4) with some success, but not as much as we had hoped for.

This chapter will provide a range of tried and tested drills that develop the core components of conditioning – speed, power and aerobic endurance. They can be used as the basis of your conditioning sessions, and can be used at any time during the yearly conditioning cycle.

This chapter will cover:

- A brief introduction to the drills – how they should be used and specific guidelines for use with amateur and junior players.
- My top 50 conditioning drills.
- A brief look at using gym work as part of the conditioning programme.

Using the drills

These drills have been tried and tested by the first team, reserves and Academy players (9–19-year-olds) over the last ten years or so. They offer a wide range of variety, ranging from short ten-minute sessions (mainly speed drills between warm-up and football training) to longer 40–50-minute conditioning sessions.

I have included drills with and without the ball, some swimming pool conditioning sessions (of which we do a lot, especially for injured players) and covered several upper body medicine ball drills. For many of the drills I have set standards for sets and repetitions, with a rough guide of the timescale for completion of each repetition, which can easily be adapted. Each drill also contains a brief guideline on the time of the year when it is best used, and whether it is suitable for young players.

Conditioning with or without the ball

The debate on whether aerobic/anaerobic conditioning (running) should be done with or without a ball has been long-running. Some managers and coaches prefer this physical component to be done without a ball, others prefer it to be done with one.

I have heard some managers and coaches say that doing all the conditioning with a ball sounds great, but that it does make it possible for some lazy players to 'hide' in such drills and not make maximum effort. Also, if you play small-sided games (three-a-side or four-a-side) then the chances of getting injured increase.

The opposite of this is that some managers and coaches believe that conditioning with the ball is more relevant, that it helps to improve a player's skills (especially when they are tired), it takes the player's mind off the running and can give them an end product, e.g. dribbling, shooting, passing, etc.

For me, the first consideration is who you are working with and what is the aim of the session. For example, if you are working with children and you wish to do some conditioning, say aerobic interval running, I would suggest doing this session with a ball. This is because of the limited time available, and it will also help improve the children's skill level while under pressure. However, if you are working with adults, you might wish to assess their physical and mental state (and whether they want to push themselves to the limit) without such variables as ball control, which will naturally differ between individuals. Therefore, I suggest taking the session without a ball.

Other considerations to bear in mind when deciding whether to do a session with or without the ball are the players' attitude and mentality, the equipment available, the time allocated and the location.

Don't make training predictable

For me, the key to a successful conditioning session is variety and freshness to keep the players interested and guessing – don't make training, especially conditioning, predictable. Therefore, I prefer to mix it up, depending on with whom I am working. Sometimes I take seniors, reserves or even Academy players to a local gym (treadmills) or to a different location (river runs) just to get them away from the training ground and to give them variety. However, during the early stages of the season, particularly pre-season, I tend to do a lot of conditioning work with the ball, depending on the manager's and coach's ideology. Therefore, I have included drills both with and without a ball.

Adapting the drills

All the drills in this section can be used by semi-professional and amateur players of all levels, from Conference non-league football to Sunday teams. There is no reason not to do all of them, providing that you have the correct facilities and equipment. As we have mentioned previously, you will need to modify the drills to the level that you are coaching (in terms of both fitness and ability). Depending on the level of fitness, you need to reduce the sets and repetitions and/or give between 10–20% extra time to complete drills.

For children, the emphasis must be on giving them a taste and experience of some of the exercises while instilling in them some competitive spirit and mental strength. I suggest, for appropriate exercises, a reduction of approximately 30% in reps and sets, and that time standards are kept highly flexible. You also need to use your common sense; do not be afraid to increase the rest/recovery times between sets and reps, if necessary. I have indicated which drills are suitable for children by using the key system.

Many of the relay and sprint sessions may be relevant depending on age and equipment, etc. All quick-feet work and techniques with children are excellent. Post-growth spurt children, especially 15–16-year-olds, may start to have a taste of some of the aerobic endurance drills.

When to use the drills

As a basic guideline, the drills can be done at any time of the season, depending on fixtures and the needs of the team and the individual. However, there are times of the season when certain types of drills work particularly well:
- Aerobic (with or without a ball) – pre-season to February.
- Speed – any time during the season (avoid week one and two of pre-season).
- Speed endurance – the first three quarters of the season.
- Strength work – any time, especially the first part of the season.

I do not recommend that you use any of the aerobic or speed endurance drills in the last six to eight weeks of the season in the formats that I have suggested. However, if you are keen to use such a drill, consider reducing the duration, effort level, etc., by about 20% and it should be fine.

Key-coded system
- A   Suitable for pre-adolescent children.
- B   Suitable for post-adolescent children and adults.
- C   With-a-ball drill.
- D   Without-a-ball drill.
- E   Aerobic drill.
- F   Speed drill.
- G   Speed endurance drill.

1.

Speed endurance – without a ball

Purpose:	speed endurance with turns at varying distances
Equipment:	discs, approximately 15
Duration:	approximately 20–25mins
Sets and reps:	4–6 reps. 3 sets. 3mins active rest between sets
Participants:	minimum of 2, maximum number unlimited
Key:	B, D, G

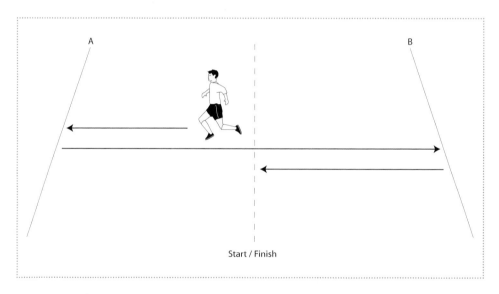

A   B

Start / Finish

Player sprints to A, then to B, and then sprints back to the start/finish. Thirty-second rest between reps. Active rest should be head tennis, ideally 2 v 2. Ensure players are working flat-out during the speed endurance drill.

2. Figure-of-8 runs

Purpose:	Aerobic interval training using the dimensions of the pitch, without a ball
Equipment:	4 cones or poles
Duration:	depending on which drill, 20–40mins
Sets and reps:	see below
Participants:	see below
Key:	B, D, E

Pre-/early season	Mid-season – Half pitch	End of season – penalty
80–85secs per rep. 60–90secs rest between reps. 3 sets of 3–4 reps. 2–3mins active rest between sets. Maximum participants 30.	42–45secs per rep. Approximately 60–70secs rest between reps. 3 sets of 4 reps. 2mins active rest between sets. Maximum participants 20.	21–23secs per rep. Approximately 60 secs rest between reps. 3 sets of 4 reps. Should be done with 2 players at a time, start from opposite sides D and A doing a figure of 8. Maximum participants 8.

Running can be done in groups of 4–6 with 10secs gaps between each group.

Player starts at A, runs to/around B, runs around C, around D and finishes back at start.

3. Aerobic interval training with a ball

(Heart monitor work, working approximately 90% of maximum)

Purpose:	Aerobic interval training with ball and turns
Equipment:	8 discs per pair working, e.g. 10 players working, 40 discs, 1 ball per player
Duration:	30–40mins
Sets and reps:	4 reps per set, 4–8 sets
Participants:	players working in pairs. Minimum of 2, maximum depends on equipment available
Key:	B, C, E

Rep 1 – Player runs with the ball to A and leaves the ball at A. (His partner is working in the opposite half, therefore he runs with the ball to E and leaves it at E.) Both players then turn, run 20m and pick up their partner's ball, turn and run back with the ball to the start position. Rest for 30–40secs.

Rep 2 – As above but working to B and F respectively.

Rep 3 – As above but working to C and G respectively.

Rep 4 – As above but working to D and H, respectively.

4–6 sets of reps. 3mins active rest, which must be head tennis in pairs. The emphasis is on quality with the ball especially when the player is tired.

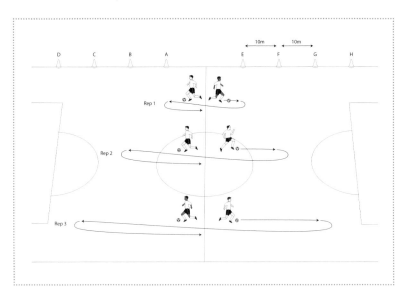

4.

Speed drill – clock face sprints without a ball

Purpose:	reaction speed drills. Also being alert and bright
Equipment:	12 discs set in a circle
Duration:	more or less 10mins, it's flexible
Sets and reps:	6–12 sprints each player
Participants:	ideally in multiples of four, e.g. 4, 8, 12, 16, 20
Key:	A, B, D, F

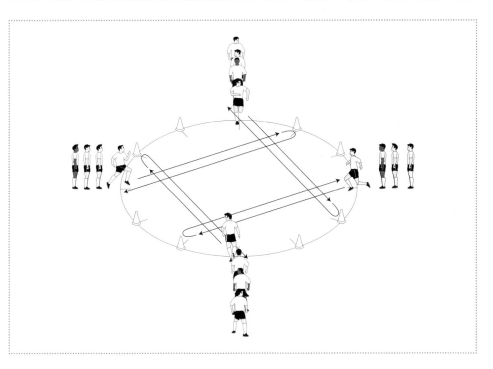

Players are marked as above. Players from each group take turns. A circle is marked as a clock face. Players are all at 12 o'clock in their 4 respective groups; therefore, directly opposite is 6 o'clock, or 3 cones to the left is 3 o'clock, etc.

The coach shouts a number, e.g. 4 o'clock (as shown in the diagram). The player sprints to 4 o'clock, sprints back to the starting position; last one back does 5 press-ups, etc.

There are many variations to this; it can be done with a ball.

5.

Aerobic/anaerobic agility work – with a ball

Purpose:	ball and multi-directional work
Equipment:	for 20 players – 10 discs, 11 cones, 10 balls
Duration:	minimum 10mins
Sets and reps:	4–10 reps, flexible
Participants:	in twos, minimum of 12 players, maximum of 20
Key:	B, C, E

S = Players serving

• = Disc

X = Players working

You will need even numbers for this drill, between 12–20. With smaller numbers the drill becomes more anaerobic, with larger numbers it becomes aerobic.

Half the squad are servers, the other half are opposite, standing next to the disc. Servers all have balls (have spares ready). On the word go, the server throws the ball to his opposite partner who then volleys it back to the server (servers stay where they are). The partner then moves right and backwards, and goes around the traffic cone to the next disc to volley again (different server). When the partner reaches the end line, he runs to the beginning and continues to volley and run until he ends up opposite his original partner (10 volleys, 10 agility runs and 1 long run). Swap servers and repeat.

Change skill to headers, passes, right and left volleys, half-volleys, sit-ups and headers, etc.

6.

Aerobic interval training – with a ball

(using heart monitors working 80–85% of maximum)

Purpose:	aerobic conditioning with a ball that includes dribbling, passing and running
Equipment:	1 ball, 6 cones or discs per pair
Duration:	approximately 24mins
Sets and reps:	4 sets of 5 reps, see below. 2mins rest between sets
Participants:	even numbers, no limits
Key:	B, C, E

Working in pairs; one works, the other rests; 1 ball between pairs. Distance between cones is approximately 8–12m.

Rep 1 – First player runs with the ball to B, stops and leaves it there. He then turns around, runs to A (without the ball), touches the cone and runs back to B, turns with the ball and passes it to his partner at A, who repeats the drill. First player jogs back after passing the ball.

Rep 2 – Once his partner has returned the ball, the first player runs with the ball to C, stops and leaves it there. He then turns around, runs to A (without the ball), touches the cone and runs back to C, turns with the ball and passes it to his partner at A, who repeats the drill. First player jogs back, after passing the ball.

Rep 3 – Repeat as above but working to D.

Rep 4 – Repeat as above but working to E.

Rep 5 – Repeat as above but working to F.

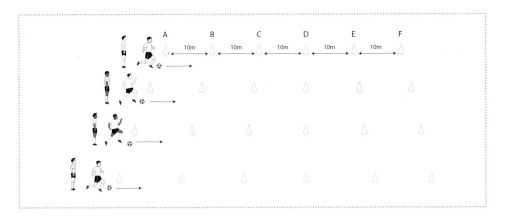

7. Box to box – without the ball

Purpose:	aerobic interval training using the dimensions of the pitch
Equipment:	none
Duration:	approximately 20–24mins
Sets and reps:	4 sets, 6–8 reps
Participants:	unlimited
Key:	B, D, E

Subject to the dimensions of the pitch; Working 85–90% effort. Box to box should take approximately 11secs. The width of penalty box recovery runs should be approximately 22–25secs (slow jog).

Players can work in small groups.

Allows 2mins recovery between sets, the last minute of which must be with a ball (keep ball up, etc.).

The player starts at A and runs to B in 11secs. Then from B he jogs to C in 22–25 secs. At C he runs to D in 11secs. Then from D he jogs to A in 22–25secs. Repeat this 6–8 times.

8.

Sprint relay – competitive with a ball

Beware of cheats!

Purpose:	speed work, in a competitive relay, also a bit of fun
Equipment:	1 ball, 3 mannequins, 1 cone per relay line
Duration:	several minutes+
Sets and reps:	flexible, suggest approximately 6 sprints per player
Participants:	flexible, due to relay format
Key:	A, B, C, F

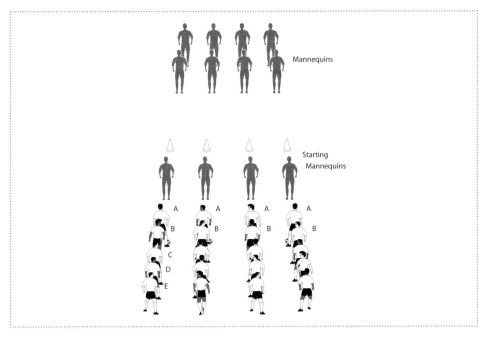

Distance between cones and mannequins your choice

1 ball per group

Player A runs with the ball to the cone and stops the ball dead. He does a figure of 8 around the mannequin and then passes the ball to B. B must take the ball and himself (prevents cheating) behind the starting mannequin and repeat the drill. The relay finishes when E passes the ball back to A and sprints past the starting mannequin.

There are many variations to this, depending on ball skills, requirements, etc.

9.

Anticipation sprint drills – without a ball

Purpose:	competitive sprint drill, relay, anticipation being the key
Equipment:	4 poles per team. Poles must only be shoulder-width apart
Duration:	several mins
Sets and reps:	flexible, suggest approximately 6–10 sprints per player
Participants:	various due to relay format, minimum of 8 (2 teams of 4)
Key:	A, B, D, F

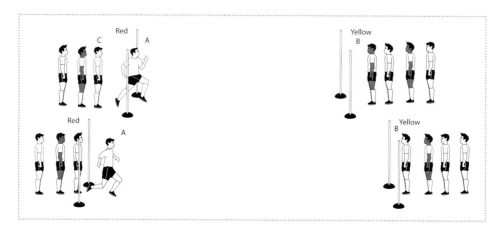

- Two red poles (shoulder-width apart only), two yellow poles (shoulder-width apart), red and yellow poles 15m–20m apart in a straight line.

Relay race, 2 sprints per race so each player ends where he started.

Four players line up at each end, approx. 2m behind the red or yellow poles, and at a diagonal angle. Player A sprints from starting point through red poles to the yellow poles opposite. As he runs between yellow poles, player B immediately sprints through them in the opposite direction, having anticipated player A's passing through the yellow poles and perfectly timed his run from his own starting point (this is critical). As player B passes through the red poles at the opposite end, player C goes through in the opposite direction having anticipated player B's arrival, and so on until every player has done 2 sprints.

Poles must not be knocked down.

Change the distance between red/yellow poles between sets.

10.

Interval training – without a ball
(Heart rate monitors working 90% of maximum)

Purpose:	working in pairs, interval training using different length of runs and rest periods between reps
Equipment:	6 cones per pair
Duration:	20–30mins
Sets and reps:	working for 3min periods, 2mins active rest, 4–6 sets
Participants:	minimum of 2 players, working in pairs
Key:	B, D, E

Four players at the starting position, split and working in pairs.

The first pair is Player 1 and Player 2, running in opposite directions but at the same time.

Player 1 runs to A, touches the top of the cone and runs to B, touches the top of the cone and runs back to the start. At the same time Player 2 runs to B, touches the top of the cone and runs to A, touches the top of the cone and runs back to the start.

When first pair returns, the second pair goes. When second pair returns, the first pair do the second stage, which is:

Player 1 runs to C, touches the cone and runs to D, touches the cone and runs back to the start. At the same time Player 2 runs to D, touches the cone and runs to C, touches the cone and runs back to the start.

When the first pair returns, the second pair goes. When the second pair returns, the first pair do the third stage of drill, which is:

As above but working to E and F respectively and so on.

Repeat the drill for 3mins.

You can make this drill into a multi-directional workout if you wish, by changing the position of the cones.

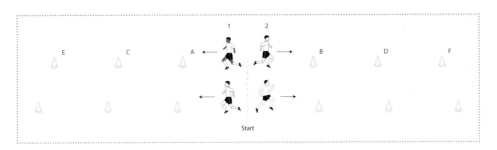

11. Aerobic interval training – treadmill work

Purpose:	cross-training on a treadmill, introduces variety
Equipment:	treadmills, 1 per player
Duration:	25mins
Sets and reps:	see below
Participants:	one player per treadmill
Key:	D, E

Note: treadmill work tends to be between 10–15% easier than running outside. Difficulty can be increased by putting up the incline by 1% if you wish.

5mins warm-up on the treadmill and 5mins stretching.

1.	0–3mins	at	12.0kph
2.	3–5mins	at	14.0kph
3.	5–6mins	at	15.0kph
4.	6–6.5mins	at	16.0kph
5.	6.5–7mins	at	12.0kph
6.	7–7.5mins	at	16.5kph
7.	7.5–8mins	at	12.0kph
8.	8–8.5mins	at	17.0kph
9.	8.5–9.5mins	at	12.0kph
10.	9.5–10mins	at	18.0kph
11.	10–12mins	at	13.0kph
12.	12–12.5mins	at	18.5kph
13.	12.5–13mins	at	12.0kph
14.	13–13.5mins	at	19.0kph
15.	13.5–14mins	at	12.0kph
16.	14–14.5mins	at	20.0kph
17.	14.5–15mins	at	12.0kph
18.	15–15.5mins	at	20.0kph
19.	15.5–16mins	at	12.0kph
20.	16–16.5mins	at	20.0kph
21.	16.5–17mins	at	12.0kph
22.	17–20mins	at	14.0kph
23	20–23mins	at	12.0kph
24.	23–25mins	at	10.0kph

❶ 22 changes of pace.

❷ Just stick this programme on the treadmill and follow the guidelines.

❸ Use your heart rate as a guideline, i.e. at 20kph your heart rate should be just below max–change pace accordingly.

12.

Sprint races – competitive, without a ball

Purpose:	to improve players' speed in a competitive environment
Equipment:	2 mannequins and 1 cone per pair
Duration:	flexible, 10mins
Sets and reps:	6–8 sprints per player, working to a minimum of 1:4 ratio
Participants:	unlimited, depending on equipment
Key:	A, B, D, F

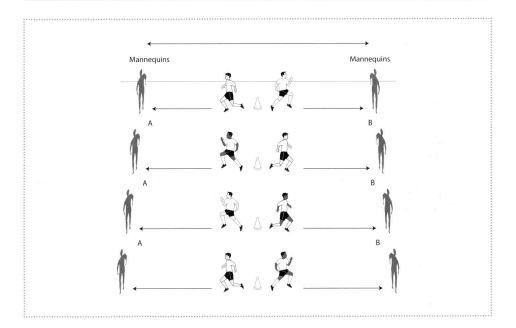

Players start and finish at the traffic cones – the starting position is touching the traffic cone.

On the word go (or at the drop of a ball), one player sprints to mannequin A, the other to mannequin B. Both players touch the mannequins and sprint past the cones to finish.

Try to work to a minimum of 1:4 ratio.

Adaptation 1	As above but around mannequins.
Adaptation 2	Touch mannequin A, then sprint and touch mannequin B and sprint past the cone to the finish.
Adaptation 3	As adaptation 2 but go around the mannequins.

13. Sprint races – competitive, without a ball

Purpose:	to improve the players' speed in a competitive environment
Equipment:	4 mannequins, 1 cone per player
Duration:	flexible, approximately 10mins
Sets and reps:	flexible, suggest several sprints each player
Participants:	must be even numbers, minimum of 8
Key:	A, B, D, F

Performed mainly with small groups.

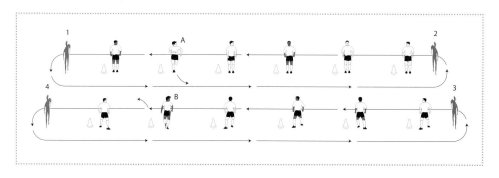

Each player facing partner on traffic cone.

When the coach shouts the player's name, he and his partner turn to the left, sprint around the mannequin, sprint to the other mannequin and around it, then sprint to starting position.

i.e. A sprints around mannequin 2 and 1, then back to the start (see diagram).

B sprints around mannequin 4 and 3, then back to the start.

All players are jogging on the spot awaiting their names or partner's name.

The distance between the mannequins is your choice, depending on the number and age of the players.

14.   Agility interval training – with a ball

Purpose:	agility interval training, mirroring in a defending posture/motion
Equipment:	1 ball per pair
Duration:	approx 25–30mins
Sets and reps:	4 reps to a set (2 dribbles each player). 4–6 sets, rest 2mins between sets
Participants:	unlimited, must be in pairs
Key:	B, C, E

This drill mirrors a defending posture and motion.

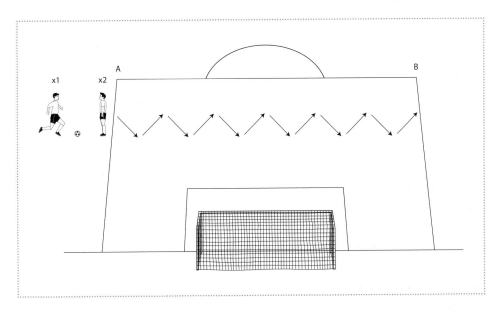

Work the width of a penalty box in pairs. One ball per pair. Players x¹ and x² are facing each other approximately 1m apart across the whole width of the penalty box. Player x¹ has the ball A and dribbles the ball to B. Player x², staying approximately 1m away, mirrors x¹. When x¹ dribbles with his right foot x² 'shows' him the outside line; when x¹ dribbles with his left foot, x² shows him the inside line. Player x¹ changes lead feet approximately 6 times. When both players reach B, both players jog back to A with the ball. When they reach A, players swap over and repeat the exercise.

15.

Interval/agility training – with a ball

Purpose:	aerobic interval training with a ball; includes passing, dribbling, agility and change of pace
Equipment:	2 mannequins and 2 cones + 1 ball per line
Duration:	24mins
Sets and reps:	2 teams, 4mins work, 4mins rest as server
Participants:	must be even numbers; minimum 8, maximum 16
Key:	C, E

Drill based on players working at 85% of maximum heart rate (heart rate monitors required).

S = Server

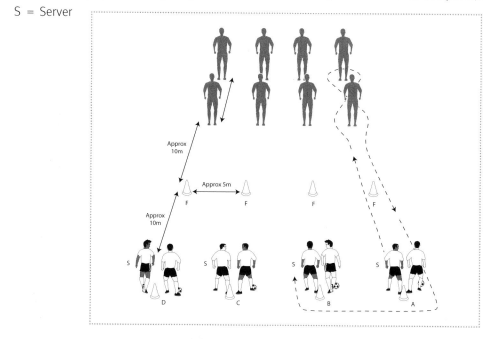

Working in pairs, the server and player working alternately, 4mins each.

First player dribbles and stops the ball at cone player, then (without a ball) increases his pace and does a figure of 8 around the mannequins, returns to cone F and passes the ball accurately to the server. The player then runs around server/cone A, around server/cone B, picks up the ball and repeats. End of line D runs to A to repeat the drill. This is continuous for approximately 24mins (4mins work, 4mins as server).

16.

Speed reaction drill – without a ball, reacting to colours

Purpose:	speed reaction drill, reacting to colours; includes turns
Equipment:	approximately 8–10 mannequins and a minimum of 5 coloured cones
Duration:	flexible, approximately 10mins
Sets and reps:	flexible, 6–8 sprints each; ratio of 1:5
Participants:	unlimited
Key:	A, B, D, F

C = Coach

The distance between the mannequins is your choice.

Place 4–6 coloured discs next to each mannequin; for example, line A has yellow, red and blue, and line B has white and green discs.

Players line up facing the coach (C). The coach produces a coloured disc from behind his back, the players then reacting to the colour by sprinting to the relevant mannequin, touching it with a foot and sprinting back to the start position.

There are many, many variations on this.

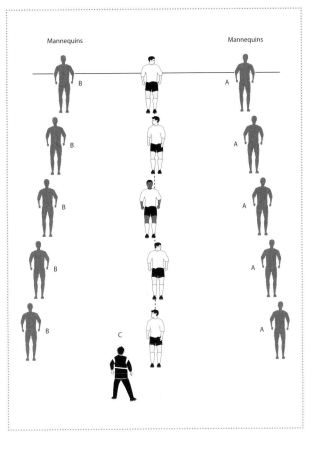

17.

Interval/recovery training – with or without a ball

Purpose: aerobic interval training, with or without a ball, with different recovery periods between each run

Equipment: none if without a ball; 2 balls per group of 3 players

Duration: subject to needs. Suggest 12mins to 32mins

Sets and reps: see below for reps. 3–8 sets

Participants: must be in groups of three, unlimited.

Key: B, C or B, D, E

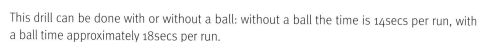

This drill can be done with or without a ball: without a ball the time is 14secs per run, with a ball time approximately 18secs per run.

The run is the width of the penalty box and back. Two players run, 1 player rests.

Players A and B run the width of the penalty box and back in 14secs. Wait for 5secs.

Players B and C do the same run. Wait for 5secs.

Finally players A and C do the same run, which completes the first set.

On each set, change the order in which the players run, i.e. rep 2 – first run A and C, second run A and B, third run B and C.

Rep 3 – first run B and C, second run A and C, third run A and B. This completes 1 set. Rest between sets is 60secs.

Now go back to the original order for the start of next set.

Complete 12–32mins work (subject to needs).

18. Agility work – head tennis, 2 v 2

Purpose:	not only works ball skills, but if done correctly works anticipation, reaction, agility and speed
Equipment:	some sort of barrier (net) and discs. 1 ball per team
Duration:	flexible
Sets and reps:	flexible
Participants:	multiples of 4, e.g. 4, 8, 12, 16 etc.
Key:	A, B, C, F

Small net or gym benches. The court size depends on the width of the benches/nets, etc., approximately 6–7m length by approximately 2–3m width.

There are many variations to this, use the coaches' input. My favourite is one touch per player; once each player has had a touch, both must touch the top of the net/bench and get ready to receive the ball.

The opposition must both touch the ball and they must both touch the net/bench and return to their position before they can receive the ball again.

This is excellent for agility, reaction, speed-of-thought and movement.

19.

Aerobic interval training – without a ball

Purpose:	aerobic interval training using the dimensions of a pitch
Equipment:	4 cones or poles
Duration:	25–30mins
Sets and reps:	4–6 reps, 4–5 sets
Participants:	unlimited
Key:	D, E

Heart monitors worn, working 80–90%

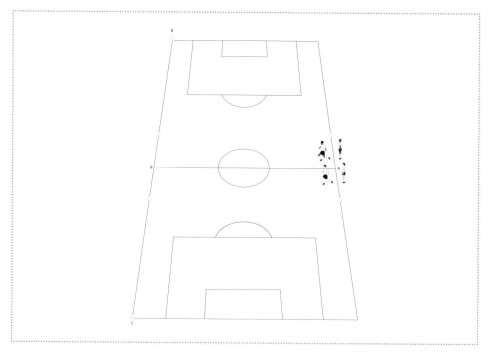

Players are split into groups. Two groups go at a time. Players start at A and jog slowly down to B. One group then goes around the cone, turns left and strides to and around cone C, then strides back to the starting position. The second group does the same run, running the other half of the pitch (A to B to D to A). On return to A, the groups swap position; therefore the first group now does A to B to D to A and vice-versa. Depending on the size of the pitch, this run takes 16–25secs. Rest between sets is approx 2–3mins active rest, i.e. head tennis.

20.

Speed endurance – without ball, working at maximum

Purpose:	to improve players' speed endurance
Equipment:	cones
Duration:	16–24mins
Sets and reps:	4 runs = 1 set, 4–6sets
Participants:	unlimited
Key:	D, G

Jog 5 metres and then sprint 30m

Jog 5 metres and then sprint 35m

Jog 5 metres and then sprint 40m

Jog 5 metres and then sprint 45m

$\left.\vphantom{\begin{array}{c}1\\2\\3\\4\end{array}}\right\}$ (4 runs equal 1 set)

Walk for 2mins between sets.

21.

Speed endurance – without ball, working at maximum

Purpose: to improve players' speed endurance
Equipment: cones
Duration: 18–20mins
Sets and reps: 4 runs = 1 set, total of 4 sets
Participants: unlimited
Key: D, G

Sprint half a pitch; rest 25secs
Sprint half a pitch; rest 20secs } 4 runs equal 1 set
Sprint half a pitch; rest 15secs
Sprint half a pitch

4 sets

Rest 1min after 1st set

Rest 1mins 30secs after 2nd set

Rest 2mins after 3rd set

22.

Frappier Acceleration/power sports training – on treadmills

Purpose:	to develop speed and power using an alternative training method, treadmill work
Equipment:	1 treadmill per 3 or 4 players
Duration:	40–50mins
Sets and reps:	see below
Participants:	3 or 4 players per treadmill
Key:	D, G

(Developed by Frappier Acceleration sports training.) The following 2 programmes are an adaptation of one component of Frappier Acceleration, which has proved to be very successful and popular with players.

Overall, with trial and error, we have developed 6 of our own specific programmes for our needs.

Warm-up and stretch for 20mins. Focus on athletes 'cycling' the legs and using full ROM (range of movement) of hamstrings and quads.

Stretch the hamstrings, quads and calves after each run.

NO.	SPEED km	SETS	% ELEV	TIME
1.	12.0	2	5	30secs
2.	12.0	1	7.5	20secs
3.	12.0	1	10	10secs (Hold)
4.	15.0	1	10	10secs (Hold)
5.	15.0	2	10	8secs
6.	15.0	2	12	8secs
7.	16.5	2	12	8secs
8.	16.5	2	12	8secs Run/8secs Hold/8secs Run
9.	17.0	1	12	6–8secs
10.	18.0	1	12	6–8secs
11.	19.0	1	12	6–8secs
12.	19.0	2	0	10secs

Players must first learn how to mount/dismount a moving inclined treadmill.

Players work in groups of 3 or 4 per treadmill. One works, the others rest.

When recovering between runs, players must stretch.

On hold, the players hold the front of the treadmill; the emphasis is on the cycle motion of running.

Ensure the players have a good warm-up before the session and cool-down after.

23.

Frappier Acceleration/power sports training – on treadmills

Purpose:	to develop speed and power using an alternative training method, treadmill work
Equipment:	1 treadmill per 3 or 4 players
Duration:	40–50mins
Sets and reps:	see below
Participants:	3 or 4 players per treadmill
Key:	D, G

See Drill 22 – Frappier Programme (Adaptation).

Warm-up and stretch for 20mins. Focus on athletes 'cycling' the legs and using the full ROM of hamstrings and quads.

Stretch the hamstrings, quads and calves after each run.

NO.	SPEED km	SETS	%ELEV	TIME
1	12.0	2	5	30secs
2	12.0	1	10	20secs
3	15.0	2	12	15secs
4	15.0	2	12	10secs (Hold)
5	15.0	2	12	10secs
6	16.5	2	12	10secs (Hold)
7	16.5	2	15	8secs Run/8secs Hold/8secs Run
8	18.0	1	15	8secs
9	19.0	4	15	6secs
10	20.0	2	15	6secs run
11	20.0	1	0	6–8secs

24. Sprint relay – competitive with rugby ball

Beware of cheats!

Purpose:	to improve players' speed in a competitive environment using a rugby ball, and having a bit of fun
Equipment:	3 mannequins, 1 cone, 1 rugby ball per relay line
Duration:	flexible, approximately 10mins
Sets and reps:	flexible, suggest 4–8 sprints
Participants:	minimum 6 (2 relay lines), maximum unlimited (subject to equipment)
Key:	A, B, F

The distance between mannequins and cones is your choice. On the drop of a ball by the coach, the first player holding the rugby ball sprints to the 2 mannequins at A, completes a figure of 8 and does a diving rugby throw to his team-mate, who then must go behind mannequin B with the rugby ball and repeat drill. Sprint relay is completed after the last man throws rugby ball to the first player.

There are dozens of variation on this.

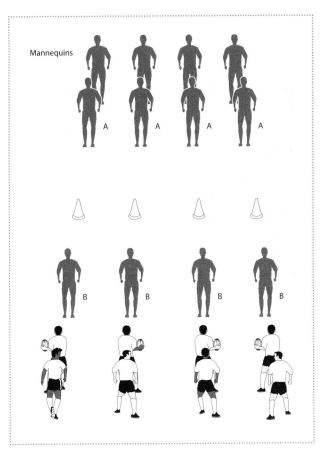

25. Quick-feet speed drill – anticipation and reaction work

Purpose:	quick-feet drill to develop several components of speed, quick feet, anticipation and reaction
Equipment:	4 ladders
Duration:	flexible, approximately 10mins
Sets and reps:	flexible
Participants:	minimum 12, maximum 24
Key:	A, B, D, F

Based on ladder work.

Ladders are positioned as shown in the diagram.

Players are positioned in equal numbers behind the ladders as shown. The centre of the exercise is marked A. The area must be relatively tight, i.e. 3m x 3m. All drills depend on the foot pattern drills the conditioner wishes to use. One player in each group goes at the same time. Halfway through the ladder drill, the player steps

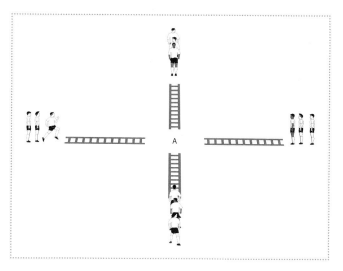

out of the ladder and sprints to the opposite ladder and rests. As soon as the player steps out of the ladder, the second player of each group goes, etc. Players must sprint when out of the ladder and be aware of other players sprinting, hence anticipation, reaction and agility.

There are many variations on this, not only for pattern drills, but with the ladder being replaced with e.g. poles, cones, mannequins.

26. Quick feet – speed, drill anticipation and reaction work with a ball

Purpose:	quick-feet drill to develop several components of speed, quick feet, anticipation, reaction and visual awareness
Equipment:	4 ladders and 1 ball
Duration:	flexible, approximately 10mins
Sets and reps:	flexible
Participants:	minimum 12, maximum 24
Key:	A, B, C, F

As drill 25 but with a bigger centre A, approximately 8m x 8m and a ball at the end of one ladder. This drill is subject to the chosen foot pattern drill. One player in each group goes at the same time and goes through the whole ladder. When the player reaches the end of the ladder, the player with the ball passes it to any other player, who is in the centre. He then sprints to the end of another ladder and waits his turn. As soon as each player passes the ball, the next person on his ladder starts his run through. If this is done at pace; the player with the ball will always have an option to pass the ball. The player who passes the ball must always sprint to the group with the least players, promoting visual awareness.

Variations on this include keeping the ball off the ground.

27.

Sprint agility in pairs – with ball skills

Purpose:	competitive sprint agility work, working with balls
Equipment:	minimum of 2 mannequins, 6 traffic cones and 2 balls
Duration:	flexible, 10–15mins
Sets and reps:	flexible, 4–8 sprints each player; work to a minimum ratio 1:4
Participants:	minimum of 4 players, maximum depends on equipment available
Key:	A, B, C, F

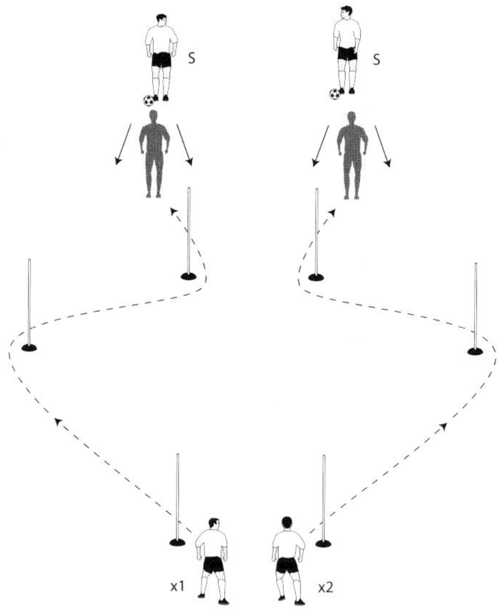

S = Server with ball

X = Players

Distance optional.

Two players, x¹ and x², race each other as shown in the diagram. When they reach the server they must complete two passes, either side of the mannequin. When the second pass is complete, they turn and race back to the start.

This exercise can de adapted in many ways. Just use your imagination.

28.

Speed agility – with ball

Purpose:	competitive sprint agility work, working with balls
Equipment:	4 cones, 1 mannequin, 1 ball per group
Duration:	flexible, 10–15mins
Sets and reps:	flexible, between 4–8 sprints per player; work ratio 1:2
Participants:	3 players per group; maximum unlimited, depending on equipment available
Key:	A, B, C, F

S = Server with ball

Four cones are are arranged in a square approximately 6m x 6m.

Player X starts by completing 2 passes either side of the mannequin. He turns and sprints to A, works laterally to B, works backwards and laterally to C, and works laterally to D, turns, goes back to the mannequin and finishes with 2 passes either side of the mannequin and starts the run again. He does this sequence twice and then swaps with a partner. The player is always facing letter E at cones.

Can be easily varied.

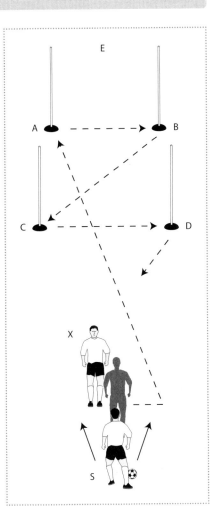

29.

Speed endurance – without a ball, work at maximum speed

Purpose:	to improve players' speed endurance
Equipment:	cones
Duration:	16mins
Sets and reps:	7 runs = one set; maximum 3 sets
Participants:	unlimited
Key:	D, G

1 × 10m sprint – walk back to start
1 × 20m sprint – walk back to start
1 × 30m sprint – walk back to start
1 × 40m sprint – walk back to start } 1 set; rest for 2mins; maximum of 3 sets
1 × 30m sprint – walk back to start
1 × 20m sprint – walk back to start
1 × 10m sprint – walk back to start

30.

Aerobic endurance

Based on Helgerud and Hoft (Norwegian University of Science and Technology)

Purpose:	to improve players' aerobic endurance in an efficient, safe manner
Equipment:	1 treadmill per player, and heart rate monitors
Duration:	32mins
Sets and reps:	see below
Participants:	unlimited, depending on treadmills available
Key:	D, E

If you can find a gym with a TV and music, players enjoy the session more.

Base the drill on a player's maximum heart rate e.g. 200; so in the 90–95% training zone this will be e.g. 180–190bpm.

Ideally, use a treadmill on a 3% incline for the whole 32min programme but the programme can be done running outside or even as a soccer circuit.

Programme:

1. 0–4mins: run fast until your heart rate reaches 90–95% of maximum and keep it in that zone until 4mins are completed (treadmill may be 16–17kph). You can decrease the speed if you are beyond 95%.

2. 4–7mins (heart rate must not go below 130bpm): Walk until your heart rate is 130 then jog slowly to keep it just above 130.

3. 7–11mins: as number 1. Note that you will reach your 90–95% max much quicker and you will end up decreasing your speed more to ensure you do not get above 95% of heart rate max.

4. 11–14mins: as number 2.

5. 14–18 mins: as number 1 and 3.

6. 18–21mins: as number 2.

7. 21–25mins: as number 1 and 3.

8. 25–29mins: as number 2 and then warm down.

Although hard at the time, your recovery should be good, therefore you should be able to do this several times a week.

31. Quick muscular endurance workout

Purpose:	simple upper body and midriff (core) circuit that can be done anytime
Equipment:	none
Duration:	12mins
Sets and reps:	see below
Participants:	unlimited
Key:	D

Do press-ups quickly but correctly.

25 sit-ups (normal)

25 press-ups

25 sit-ups (bicycle)

25 press-ups

25 sit-ups (crunch)   } 30secs rest between exercises

25 press-ups

25 sit-ups (normal)

25 press-ups

25 sit-ups (crunch)

25 dorsi raise

Increase each session by 1–2 reps to a maximum of 35.

32.

Small-sided high intensity game
Use heart rate monitors

Purpose:	aerobic conditioning in a small-sided game situation
Equipment:	2 small goals, cones and plenty of balls
Duration:	24–32mins
Sets and reps:	2–3mins work, 2mins rest, repeat 6–8 times
Participants:	6–8 outfield players, 2 goalkeepers
Key:	C, E

This drill should be run by the coaches and monitored by the fitness conditioner. All conditions of the game are decided by the coaches.

Goalkeepers are included. Set up is 3 v 3 (or 4 v 4) working 85–95% (4 teams). The intensity of the game is controlled by the heart rate readings.

Have plenty of spare balls. Make it competitive.

Work 2 or 3mins at high intensity, rest 2mins. Do this between 6–8 times for each team.

Coaches must make sure the players are continuously working around the pitch and defending/attacking.

Approximate area required is 30–40m.

There are many variations.

33. Aerobic interval training – small-sided game with multiple goals

Purpose:	aerobic conditioning in a small-sided game situation with multiple goals
Equipment:	14 poles (or cones) and discs (2 poles to make 1 goal)
Duration:	12mins
Sets and reps:	90secs–2mins work. 45secs rest, repeat for 12mins maximum
Participants:	10 players
Key:	C, E

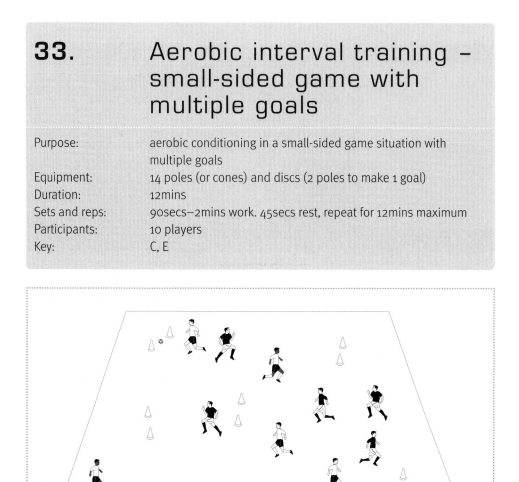

This drill should be run by the coaches and monitored by the fitness conditioner. All conditions of the game decided by coaches.

Have plenty of spare balls and use approximately one third of the pitch. Coaches must make sure that the players are working constantly around the pitch. Players must be motivated. Beware of lazy players.

Play 5 v 5 man-to-man, with 6 small-sided goals (use cones or poles). The aim is to pass the ball between the cones to a team-mate (the players cannot run through the cones). Award 1 point per pass through the goal.

34. High intensity aerobic endurance – with a ball
Use heart rate monitor

Purpose:	high intensity aerobic endurance with a ball, using game situations
Equipment:	approximately 20 poles and several balls
Duration:	28–32mins
Sets and reps:	4mins work with 2–3mins head tennis, active recovery Repeat 4–5 times
Participants:	10–12 players
Key:	C, E

Use half a pitch with poles every 15m around the perimeter. This drill should be run by the coaches and monitored by the fitness conditioner. Players must be constantly moving, hitting long and short passes.

Starting with 2 touches, having passed the ball players must run around 2 poles on the outside of the pitch and rejoin.

There are many variations to this including using two balls, changes of pace, introduction of opposition, etc.

Beware of players staying on the outside!

35. Aerobic interval training – treadmill and cross-trainer

Purpose:	cross-training, a change from normal training. Working in a gym environment
Equipment:	1 treadmill and 1 cross-trainer (or bike)
Duration:	34mins
Sets and reps:	see below
Participants:	2 per treadmill and cross-trainer
Key:	D, E

Players must learn how to mount and dismount a moving treadmill before attempting this drill.

Players work in pairs, 2mins on the treadmill and 2mins on the cross-trainer, constantly swapping. The cross-trainer should always be constant at resistance 9, 80 rpm (subject to type).

- Treadmill 14kph for 2mins and then 2mins cross-trainer (partner vice-versa).
- Treadmill 15kph for 2mins and then 2mins cross-trainer (partner vice-versa).
- Treadmill 16kph for 2mins and then 2mins cross-trainer (partner vice-versa).
- Treadmill 17kph for 2mins and then 2mins cross-trainer (partner vice-versa).
- Treadmill 18kph for 2mins and then 2mins cross-trainer (partner vice-versa).
- Treadmill 19kph for 2mins and then 2mins cross-trainer (partner vice-versa).

24min workout.

36. Swimming pool session

There are dozens of aerobic, power and anaerobic pool sessions that we can use, from team relay (anaerobic) to 24-minute aerobic sessions. All sessions depend on the swimming ability of players and the swimming pool facilities.

A simple example of a moderate intensity pool session is working in a 25m pool, 4–5ft deep. Jog in the pool for a length and swim fast (front crawl) the next length. Repeat for 18mins.

Another example of moderate intensity training is working in groups of 3, with 2 players (A and B) at one end and Player C at other end of pool. Player A swims (front crawl) to Player C and stops. When Player A arrives, Player C then swims to Player B and stops. Player B swims to A, etc. This lasts for 12–20mins.

37.

Sprint relay – competitive with batons

Watch out for dropped batons

Purpose:	to do speed work in a competitive, fun way
Equipment:	3 mannequins, 1 cone, 1 baton per relay line
Duration:	flexible, approximately 10mins
Sets and reps:	flexible 4–8 sprints
Participants:	minimum of 6, maximum unlimited, depending on equipment available
Key:	A, B, C, F

The first player sprints to mannequin C and performs a figure of 8. He then sprints back to his team-mate, who is waiting at cone B (facing in the opposite direction, back facing him) ready for handover. Once the handover is completed, the second player goes around mannequin A; repeat the drill until all players have finished.

There are many variations on this.

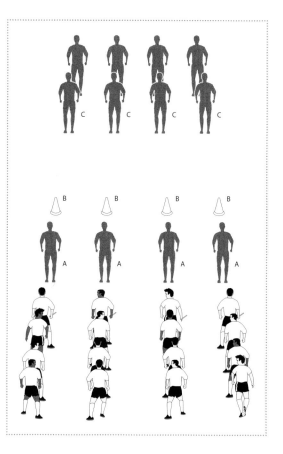

38.

Sprint drills – rolling starts
Beware of cheats!

Purpose:	to do speed drills, with rolling starts, in a competitive manner
Equipment:	10 discs and 1 ball
Duration:	flexible; approximately 10mins
Sets and reps:	flexible; suggest 4–8 sprints, working on a ratio of 1:4
Participants	minimum 3, maximum unlimited
Key:	A, B, D, F

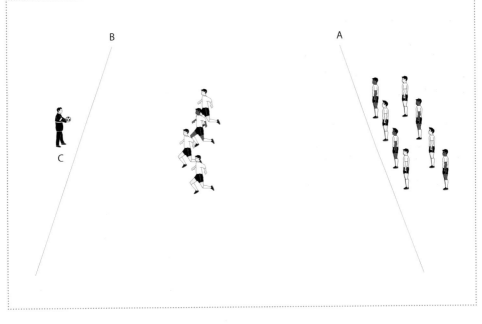

C = Coach with ball

In small groups, players start walking or jogging towards the coach. Players must be shoulder-to-shoulder. If the coach drops the ball, players sprint to the finish line B. If the coach throws the ball up in the air, players turn and sprint back to A.

Use variations on this.

39.

Aerobic endurance – pitch runs

Purpose:	aerobic endurance, using a full-sized pitch
Equipment:	4 poles
Duration:	35–40mins
Sets and reps:	run round the pitch in 60–68secs. Do 3 reps with approximately 60–70secs rest between reps. Do 3–4 sets with 2–3mins active rest between runs
Participants:	working in groups of no more than 6, maximum of 4 groups
Key:	D, E

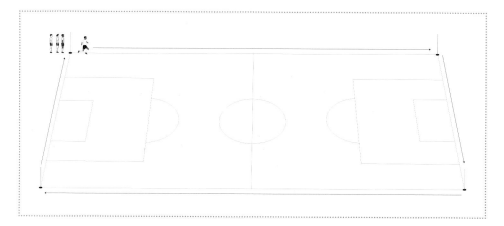

Use a full-sized pitch with poles at each corner. Depending on the size of the pitch, run around the pitch in 60–68secs. Active rest between runs, i.e. passing routine or head tennis.

40. Resisted sprint training and strength work – bungee

Over the years there have been many attempts to develop bungees which distribute the resistance/load evenly, with a harness which fits correctly and does not strain the back, or have a negative action on technique.

Depending on what type of drills, frequency and intensity required, bungee work can develop core strength, power, and technique and leg speed.

Bungee, as with most resisted training equipment, is very popular with players for three main reasons:

- It is different.
- They feel their muscles overloading quickly.
- In the contrast phase (resistance 'off' and drill repeated) they notice an immediate difference and feel good!

Whether it's bungee work, Frappier or any other resistance work, it brings variety to a session. Resistance training on a field is very dynamic and realistic to the game; you can mimic football actions and build strength while on a pitch.

The following are three of my favourite bungee drills.

40a. 20m and 30m resistance sprints and contrasts – anaerobic work

Purpose:	to develop speed and power using resistance-loaded equipment
Equipment:	discs, and one harness and bungee per two players
Duration:	approximately 15mins
Sets and reps:	4 runs each player (including contrast run) 2 sets per player (1 set to 20m, 2nd set to 30m)
Participants:	working in pairs, numbers subject to equipment
Key:	D, G

Work in pairs: 1 working and 1 resisting. On the drop of a ball, the player wearing the harness sprints to the 20m mark. The partner (who is resisting) lets the player go for 3 or 4 steps and then goes himself, keeping the resistance constant (bungee the same length).

On reaching the 20m mark, both players walk back to the start and repeat twice. After the third run, the player takes off the harness and lines up at the start. On the drop of a ball, the player then sprints to the 20m mark. The player should feel 'the speed factor' (contrast phase).

The partner now repeats above.

Repeat drill and contrast to 30m mark.

40b. 10m resistance strength runs

Purpose	to develop speed, strength and muscular endurance using resistance-loaded equipment
Equipment:	2 cones, and 1 harness and bungee per 2 players
Duration:	15–25mins
Sets and reps:	see below
Participants:	working in pairs, numbers depending on equipment
Key:	D, G

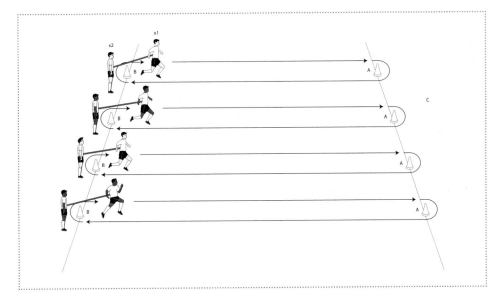

x^1 = player working

x^2 = player resisting

Player x^1 runs around cone A and then back-pedals to cone B, goes around B, and back to cone A, etc. Player x^1 is always facing C.

Player x^1 does this 3 times and swaps with x^2.

Player x^1 repeats the drill, but runs 5 times (A, around B and back) and swaps, and then 7 times and swaps. This concludes a set.

Complete 2 or 3 sets. Contrast phase on completion of each set is optional.

40c. Over-speed drill – slingshot

Purpose:	to develop over-speed using resistance-loaded equipment
Equipment:	2 cones, and 1 harness and 2 bungees per pair of players
Duration:	10–15mins
Sets and reps:	6–8 over-speed sprints each player, Working on a 1:8 ratio
Participants:	working in pairs, numbers depending on equipment
Key:	B, C, F

This drill improves stride rate, stride frequency, arm swing acceleration and reflexes. Two players work together, one resisting (x^2), the other working (x^1).

You need 2 bungee ropes tied together. On the drop of the ball both players start sprinting. Player x^2 only sprints to the 5m cone while x^1 sprints a total of 25m. Bungee ropes are at full extension at the start of the sprint drill.

Repeat this 6–8 times and then do a contrast.

41.

Aerobic interval training – athletics track

Purpose:	aerobic interval training on an athletics track with muscular endurance work for active recovery between sets
Equipment:	athletics track
Duration:	35–40m
Sets and reps:	see below
Participants:	working in groups of 4–8 players; Maximum of 4 groups
Key:	D, E

400m x 4 reps – 80secs every 400m, 60–90secs recovery between reps. 3mins' rest including 30 press-ups, 30 sit-ups, 30 dorsi raises.

300m x 6 reps – 54 secs every 300m, 60–90secs' recovery between reps. 3mins' rest including 30 press-ups, 30 sit-ups, 30 dorsi raises.

200m x 8 reps – 34secs every 200m, 60–90secs recovery between reps. Rest is active walk.

42.

High intensity interval training – athletics track, hard session

Purpose:	high intensity interval training on an athletics track (endurance work)
Equipment:	athletics track
Duration:	30mins
Sets and reps:	see below
Participants:	in groups of 4–8 players; Maximum of 4 groups
Key:	D, E

Run (high intensity) for 200m in 32secs each time.

Have approximately 60secs rest between reps (rest is active walk).

Do this for 30mins. This should work out to approximately 18 runs.

43. Interval training – aerobic with a ball
Heart rate monitors working 90%

Purpose:	aerobic and agility interval training, with a ball (using passing drills)
Equipment:	4 cones, 4 discs, and 1 or 2 balls per line
Duration:	approximately 30mins
Sets and reps:	see below
Participants:	working in groups of 3 players; Maximum depends on equipment available
Key:	B, C, E

Players x¹ and x² have a ball each. This is a simple pass, run and pass again routine. Player x¹ passes to x³ and x³ returns the ball, then turns (180°), runs, touches cones 1, 2, 3, 4 (in this sequence and always facing x²), runs to disc A, receives and passes the ball back to x² and repeats the drill, working back to x¹ (sequence on cones now 4, 3, 2, 1). More skilful players can chip/drive the ball to x¹ and x² after receiving it back from x³ each time. Have spare balls available.

Set 1   Working for 30secs for each player – resting 60secs (1:2 ratio); 1 player works, 2 players serve. Each player completes × 3

Set 2   Working 40secs (1:2 ratio work to rest) × 3

set 3   Working 50secs (1:2 ratio) × 3

set 4   Working 60secs (1:2 ratio) × 2

You can change deliveries, i.e. headers, volleys, etc.

Players should be pushing themselves hard for this drill.

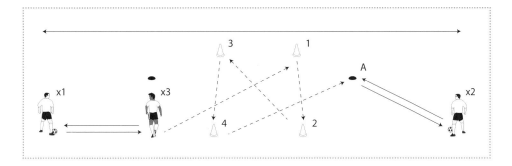

44.

Small-sided game – aerobic training, with a ball-hard session

Heart rate monitors be to worn

Purpose:	aerobic training in a small sided game, with the emphasis on breaking out in attack and recovering into defence
Equipment:	60 x 40m pitch, 2 goals, discs and plenty of balls
Duration:	maximum of 32 mins
Sets and reps:	3 or 4 mins work, rest 2 mins, repeat 3 or 4 times
Participants:	2 goalkeepers and 5 v 5 or 6 v 6
Key:	B, C, E

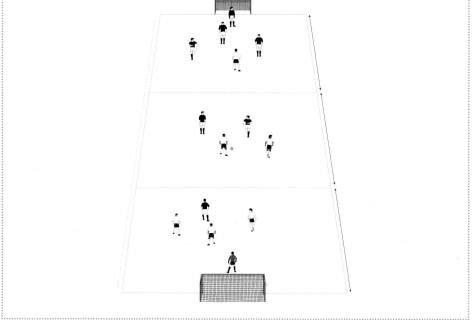

This drill should be run by the coaches and monitored by the conditioner. Coaches must ensure the game is played at high tempo.

To score a goal, all players must be in final third zone of opponents.

45.

Small-sided game – anticipation, reaction

Purpose:	aerobic training in a small-sided game, with the emphasis on a high tempo, and anticipation and reaction
Equipment:	20 × 25m pitch, 20 balls
Duration:	flexible, 15–40mins
Sets and reps:	2–3mins each game. 2 teams working, 1 resting
Participants:	3 teams of 5–6 players each
Key:	B, C, E

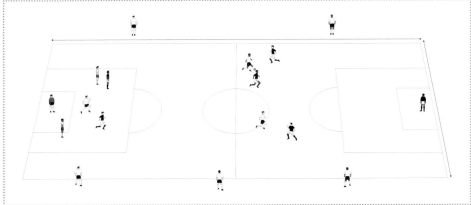

3 teams of 5 or 6; 2 playing, 1 team on outside. The 'outside' team is located around the pitch, it has one touch and can assist the team in possession.

Have plenty of balls in goal. Goalkeepers always start.

This drill is run by the coaches and monitored by the conditioner. Coaches ensure the game is played at a high tempo. The emphasis in on a quick game when a goal is scored, or a ball is out of play. Goalkeepers restart the game quickly.

46.

Speed/reaction drills – mirrors, working to a high intensity level

Purpose:	speed reaction mirroring drills, working anaerobically
Equipment:	5 × 5m box, × 2
Duration:	flexible, 5–15mins
Sets and reps:	flexible; suggest 6–10 efforts, with a 1:5 ratio.
Participants:	working in pairs; maximum subject to boxes available
Key:	A, B, C, F

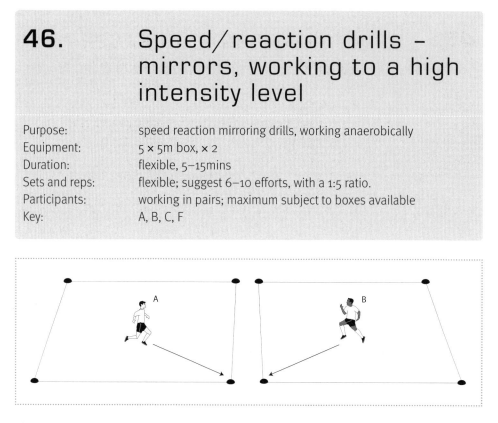

Player A will always react to B's movements. Work approximately 15–20secs, to whichever cones he moves to, etc. Players are always facing each other. Make it competitive, hence realistic. Change the rules.

47.

Multi-directional speed work

Purpose:	competitive sprint drills
Equipment:	based on 16 players, 4 mannequins and 4 cones. Ideally you need a centre circle
Duration:	flexible; 10–20mins
Sets and reps:	flexible; 6–12 sprints per player; see below; Working on approximately 1:3 ratio
Participants:	flexible; minimum 12, maximum 24 players
Key:	B, D

The distance between the mannequins and perimeter of centre circle is optional, but all must be equal.

Make runs competitive. Players face outwards as shown. Try to keep all sprints under 7–8secs.

Rep 1 – Sprints and touches the mannequin and sprints back and stops, then moves clockwise to the next station and waits for the others to finish, i.e. everybody does the same drill.

Rep 2 – Sprints and touches the mannequin, then working in a clockwise direction sprints to the next mannequin (with one foot in centre circle), touches it and sprints to station 3 and waits as per diagram.

There are many variations on this.

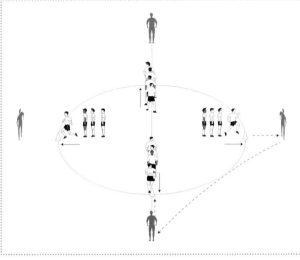

48. Multi-directional aerobic training – with a ball, moderate to hard

Purpose:	multi-directional aerobic training with a ball, using various equipment
Equipment:	ladders, cones, hurdles and balls
Duration:	20–36mins
Sets and reps:	working between 3–4mins, resting 2mins, × 4–6 times
Participants:	3 players per line; maximum depending on the equipment available.
Key:	C, E

Work 85–90% of maximum effort. Change patterns on each repetition. For example, quick feet through ladders, run in and out of poles, lateral work on cones, bounding over 6–8in hurdles, 3 passes against a bench (right, left, right) and jogging back to the beginning. Continue for 3–4 minutes.

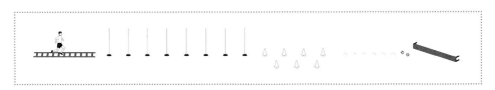

There are many variations on this.

49. Speed endurance – with a ball

Purpose:	multi-directional speed endurance, with a ball
Equipment:	4 cones, 1 ball
Duration:	24–36mins
Sets and reps:	see below; 4–6 efforts per player
Participants:	2 per square; maximum depending on the equipment available
Key:	C, G

Two players work together; one working, the other receiving the pass.

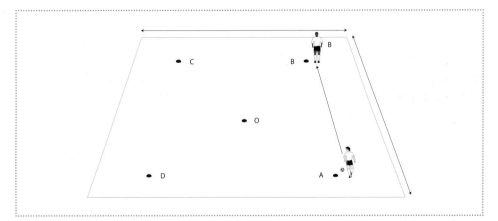

Start at A. Pass the ball to B (partner waiting at B).

Sprint A, O, A, B.

Pass the ball to C (partner waiting at C).

Sprint B, O, B, C.

Pass the ball to D (partner waiting at D).

Sprint C, O, C, D.

Pass the ball to A (partner waiting at A).

Sprint D, O, D, A.

Stop at A.

4–6 × [A, B, C, D, A (90secs) A, D, C, B, A]

90secs active rest (i.e. walking or jogging, or passing with partner).

Start at A. Pass the ball to D, then work back through C, B, A and so on (reversing drill) to finish.

Partner now goes.

50.   Small-sided game

Purpose:	aerobic, small-sided game
Equipment:	2 goals, discs and plenty of balls
Duration:	flexible, 18–24 mins
Sets and reps:	flexible, see below
Participants:	12 players and 2 goalkeepers
Key:	C, E

Two passive players from each team stand behind the goal line of their opponent's goal (one player on each side of the goal). The remaining active players play a small-sided game with normal football rules.

The exception is that they may make a wall pass to their passive team-mates who have one touch to return the ball into play. The passive players may not enter the field of play.

The number of players in each team could be:

   4 (active) + 2 (passive)

Goalkeeper and full-sized goals should be used.

2min work periods. At the end of each 2 min period, 2 of the previously active players switch places with the 2 passive players and the game is restarted (within 5secs).

In this way each player works for either 2 or 4mins and then rests (as a passive player) for 2mins.

This drill should be run by the coaches and monitored by the conditioners.

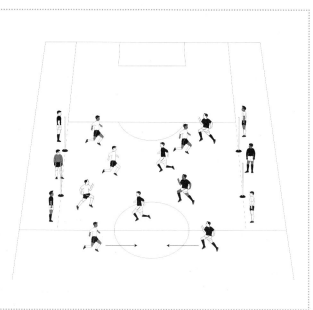

Gym work – strength training

All players should undertake a minimum basic strength programme, if only to aid general strength, prevent injury or improve self-belief and confidence. It is a foundation component of all elements of soccer from kicking a ball to holding off players. It can also be used very effectively in advanced foundation work for developing speed and sprint capabilities.

There are many excellent guides to general strength training programmes, and I do not intend to cover this ground again. Rather, this brief section will focus on the use of medicine balls in the gym. This form of strength work is often overlooked but, for me, it the best way of working with players on strength. It uses dynamic movements that reflect a player's movement on the pitch and, because it is different, it keeps training fresh and has proved to be very popular with the players. There's also the benefit that you do not need a fully equipped gym to undertake the exercises.

The first step in gym-based strength training is to teach technique and safety issues. This is true for all players (especially children), regardless of their experience. There is often a macho characteristic that comes to the surface when weights are involved – normally sensible players create all sorts of problems for themselves by trying to shift weights that are way beyond their capability.

You must convince the players that quality rules over quantity as far as weights are concerned; it is far more beneficial to complete a set of an exercise with good technique using a lighter weight/medicine ball than it is to struggle with a heavy weight with little control.

Once you've taught the techniques and safety issues, you have to ask two basic questions, regardless of what sort of programme you are putting together (whether it be static machines, free weights or medicine ball work): what is the purpose of the programme and how is it best achieved?

I prefer, especially for adult players, to do dynamic (medicine ball, boxing, power bags etc.) and free weights to develop strength. Young children should either use their own resistance of body weight or the static machines found in most health clubs.

Medicine ball work

Medicine ball work can be used either to develop general strength levels or more specific components. It is important to have a whole range of medicine ball weights from 2–3kg up to 10kg+. I once read a book which contained approximately 300 exercises (*Medicine Ball Training* by Zoltan Tenke and Andy Higgins), so the possibilities and adaptations are endless, but more importantly you can develop your own sports-specific medicine ball exercises as long as they are safe.

141

Always make sure the players use all safety procedures and have the correct weight of ball.

Basic safety procedures
- Ensure you have the correctly weighted medicine ball for the relevant exercise.
- Treat the balls with respect. I have seen top international players hurting and embarrassing themselves.
- Do not kick a medicine ball.
- Ensure you warm up, including the upper body.
- When working with medicine balls ensure you have a strong foundation and strong core position.
- When picking up a medicine ball, treat it like any other weight, bend knees, straighten back etc.

My favourite five exercises are as follows. For variation and overload, change the weights of the medicine ball, etc. All these exercises depend on the weight of the medicine ball and the age/strength level of the participants. Reps and sets are only an example.

Drop and throw

This drill develops upper body strength and power safely.

- Drill 1 – Catch, bring to chest, explode and throw ball to partner: 1 x 10, swap; 1 x 20, swap; 1 x 30, swap.
- Drill 2 – As soon as you catch it, throw the ball back up (minimum elbow bend): 1 x 10, swap; 1 x 20, swap; 1 x 20, swap.

Chest throws

Maintain a straight back; the emphasis is on core stability. Players' distance is between 2–8m.

As soon as the ball is caught, throw it back.

Power work 15 secs, rest 60secs; repeat approximately 10 times.

Repeat set with a heavy medicine ball.

Power jump

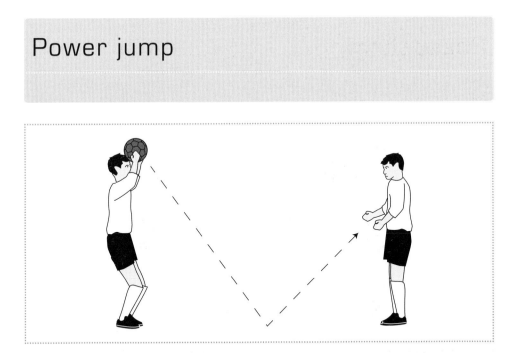

Players' distance 2m–6m. The emphasis is on strong core work. Do not let the ball go beyond the back of your head when throwing. Throw the medicine ball (with a downwards motion) two thirds of the distance between partners in an explosive manner so it bounces up.

Start with a light medicine ball and build up. 30secs work, 60secs rest. Change weights.

Variation/advanced – as the ball is thrown, jump off the floor so the power comes from the core and upper body.

Push 'n' pull

The emphasis is on strong core and back. Work with arms straight for each movement.

1 – out horizontally.

2 – back in.

3 – up vertically.

4 – back down.

Work with different weights.

Reps and sets, i.e. 2 × 12 5kg, 2 × 10 6kg, 2 × 8 7kg, 2 × 6 9kg.

Work in reps of 10, 15 or 20. Sets of 2 or 3.

Chest throws with clap press-up

The emphasis is on straight back and strong core.

As for chest throws but when the ball is thrown, quickly do a clap press-up before the partner returns the ball. Partner does the same.

Reps in 10. Rest 1min between sets. Sets × 4 to 10.

7 SECRETS OF SUCCESSFUL CONDITIONING

In this final chapter, I aim to give you some insight into what makes conditioning successful in any club – from a professional team to a Sunday-league side. Think of this chapter as a quick revision guide to how to make conditioning a key part of your team's performance.

In the following pages are my top 25 tips that I have picked up during my years in football; some are from my own research, some have been handed down from the managers and coaches I have worked with. Not all the tips will be relevant to everyone – for example, some may not work with young players. But if you take them on board you will see the difference at your club.

The Basic Principles

Whether you are a professional conditioning coach or soccer coach, an amateur soccer coach or the manager of a youth team, to deliver conditioning at your club you must follow some basic principles. These principles, which I have made into my 25 tips that I always give to coaches seeking my advice, should form the basis of your sessions. They may not all apply to every situation but they should certainly apply at some point during the season.

Your motivation, enthusiasm, knowledge and teaching skills will influence the success of a session, whether you use your skills in a warm-up or a speed endurance session. So use this book and these tips as the start of your conditioning knowledge – don't just read the book and think that's the end of it. Be sure to keep learning. Not only will it make your team better, but it will also keep the job fresh and enjoyable.

Tip 1 – The guiding principles
There are five principles that I make sure apply to every session that I take, whether it is a five-minute warm up or a full first-team speed session.

- **Do the simple things well**. Keep the sessions simple, especially at the beginning of a season, and when you are working with lots of new players who are not used to your approach. Remember what your individual players do on the pitch – running at different speeds, turning, explosive acceleration and, hopefully, enjoying themselves – and make sure that the session reflects all these elements.

- **Mix it up; keep training fresh**. There will be certain drills that, by necessity, you will have to use for most of the season, but be sure to offer variety. For example, when doing sprint drills sometimes use a rugby ball – this will force the players to think differently and also bring the upper body into play, making them adjust their usual body positioning for balance.

- **Undertake drills accurately and with specificity in mind**. Continually ask yourself the question: 'Why am I using this drill?' The players will do what you tell them; it is your responsibility to make the reasons for the session and the difference it will make to the player and the team clear. Also, to follow the advice of an old teacher of mine, 'If something is worth doing, it is worth doing properly'. Be sure that every drill is planned to the best of your ability and performed to the best of the players' abilities – only then will you see the full benefits.

- **Plan drills so that they will have a direct impact on the performance**. Go back to Chapter 1 and look at the specific demands that each player faces in his position; be sure the drills will support their performance on the pitch and reflect the demands of the game. For example, most sprints only last for a few seconds; most players work hard every 30–40 seconds at any one time, so there's little point setting off on a six-mile jog round the pitches to develop conditioning to support this.

- **Re-visit, revise and re-test when necessary**. Never take players' fitness or your knowledge for granted!

Tip 2 – Develop good theoretical knowledge

As conditioning coach or manager you are responsible for conditioning the team. This requires knowledge, so be sure to keep learning from whatever sources are available.

- **Have good basic sports science knowledge**. Read books, attend courses, speak to experts and other coaches to improve your basic knowledge.

- **Know your subject**. You need to put the theory into practice, and this will require trying out drills and programmes with the team. It may be a good idea to test some drills out on junior players, as they are often more forgiving than adults! Also, you should try out new drills before the season gets underway, or at least avoid them during key phases of the season when delivering performance is crucial. Be sure that you are comfortable with your knowledge and experience before taking the drills onto the training pitch.

- **Learn from the mistakes**. Not everything will go right every time, and don't kid yourself that it will. When a session doesn't go to plan, be sure to learn from the mistake and move on. Also, it's good to learn from other people's mistakes, so talk to other coaches and trade stories.

> 'Warm up thoroughly before training or playing. Keep to a healthy diet. And get plenty of sleep as it is essential for recovery.'
>
> *Darren Ambrose, England U21 international*

Tip 3 – Learn from the coaches

Most managers and coaches have played the game for many years and this brings a wealth of experience that can be of considerable assistance to you. Talk to them about the team and individuals, and discuss the drills that you are planning. You may be able to incorporate their feedback into your sessions.

Tip 4 – Planning

So important it has its own chapter. You will have heard it before, but that doesn't make it less true: 'Failing to plan is planning to fail.' As far as I know, there is no conditioning magic wand – success comes down to planning the whole season. You will not achieve much in a couple of sessions, but you will see results after 6–10+ sessions (depending, of course, on what you are trying to achieve). Plan your year, cycle/periods, not just daily or pre-season but throughout the season. This is applicable to all levels – amateur or professional, children or adults – that hold regular training sessions throughout the season.

Tip 5 – Prioritise

You will never be able to achieve everything you want as a conditioning coach; this is a fact of life. But a coach's job of conditioning the team is sometimes made difficult by the fact that playing football matches often gets in the way of training! So, you must prioritise your goals while taking into account any circumstances that you may not have been aware of when you set your original plans. Talk to the manager and other coaches to make sure that you are working towards the same goals and regularly review these goals to make sure that the priorities are still the correct ones.

Tip 6 – Talk to the players

Once you get to know your players, you will find there are some that you can relate to particularly well. These individuals are vital for player feedback, which should form an important part of your ongoing planning. They can also act as your 'champions' with the rest of the team, convincing others of the importance of conditioning, explaining why the team does certain drills, and encouraging players to look after their own conditioning away from the club. Always try to educate the players about the benefits of conditioning as you lead the sessions.

Tip 7 – Specialist assistance

Accept your own strengths and weaknesses and never be afraid to seek specialist help to cover one of your less strong areas. For example, I regularly use a nutritionist and yoga teacher to help with the conditioning of my players. The added benefit of different faces and voices keeps a fresh and varied approach, and it will also help to continually develop your own knowledge.

You do not have to be a professional club or have money to spare to bring in this specialist help; you will be surprised how many people are keen to get involved in football on a voluntary basis. By getting involved with the team, it gives the specialist the opportunity to try their skills out on a very different audience – our yoga teacher didn't work with so many young adult men until working at the club – and helps them to improve their knowledge. It's a win–win.

Tip 8 – Player individuality

What works for one player may not work for another; therefore, you may at times have to look at individuals more than the team. For example, some players need more rest than others, yoga may suit some players and not others, and so on. This is particularly true when working with an adult team with players covering a wide age range, or with youth teams that may have players at different levels of physical development.

Tip 9 – Player mentality

Never underestimate the importance of a player's attitude and mental approach towards conditioning, e.g. if you tell a player he is tired, he may act tired; if you tell a player he is as fit as ever, he tends to run more in a game. When a team is on a winning run this 'feel-good factor' often results in fewer injuries, etc. Tell the players the sessions you are doing can only be beneficial, etc.

Tip 10 - You are what you eat

This is a whole new subject in itself. Nutrition is a key component of performance, whether in a game or in training. It is one area where you are going to have to tailor your advice to each individual, but it also relies on players taking responsibility for their own actions away from the club. Educating the players on this matter is important; give them the basics of how to develop a healthy diet and outline what the effects of a bad diet are. You can also remind them of the testing that you can and will undertake to monitor their fitness – this can be particularly beneficial when sending players away for the close season, a time when the exercise levels tend to drop and the calorie intake increases.

Tip 11 - Lifestyle

Unsuitable outside influences have a bearing, and will affect training and eventually match-performance. Like nutrition, this is an area where you must put responsibility firmly into the players' hands and support them with education on the subject.

Tip 12 - Monitor players

Monitor players' schedules, training days and frequency of injuries, etc., and be sure to record all your results in a database. This can reveal that some players always pick up injuries in pre-season, which directly affects form. A player can get injured after a hectic period of games. I have known players who always seem to be injured on Mondays; young players who have never missed a day's training or been unavailable for a match in two and a half years; other players who suffer injury training on Astroturf while others get hamstring and calf problems on heavy pitches. By keeping a record and being proactive with conditioning you will learn to spot emerging patterns and minimise injuries.

Tip 13 - The 4Rs

Rest, Recovery, Refuelling and Re-hydration – adhere to these or see performance suffer.

Tip 14 - Reversibility

Analysis at Ipswich Town shows that, generally, players do not lose their basic aerobic conditioning for 10–28 days if injured, so long as you keep them active (depending on the type of injury). However, skill and ball work are a completely different issue! These do fall away and the player will need time to recover. Note that speed and strength tend to suffer first during a period of inactivity.

Tip 15 – Work with injured players

When a player is injured, aerobic/anaerobic fitness should be maintained by adapted cross-training (subject to the type of injury). Depending on the injury and a few days' post-injury rest, most players can participate in cycling, cross-training, swimming or weights, or a combination of these. As the conditioner, you are aiming to maintain fitness levels (work with the physio). This, in the long term, is very important.

TRAINING MYTH

'Long-distance runs are an excellent way of training players.'

Although long-distance running has many benefits, soccer training must be specific to the demands of the game and to the position of the player. In a game, when does a player go on a four- or five-mile run, non-stop, at a constant pace, without turning, changing direction or jumping? Soccer is a multi-directional, multi-paced game.

Tip 16 – Be realistic

Do not promise what cannot be achieved. You can make players quicker, but you cannot make all players into Thierry Henry! You can make players stronger for football, but you cannot and will not make them into weightlifters. Not only is this important for the players in terms of managing their expectations, but it also ensures that you play to the actual strengths and weaknesses of the team, not some unrealistic ideal.

Tip 17 – Testing

There are numerous tests that can be undertaken but reality shows you need to plan which tests you are going to do and when to repeat them, bearing in mind time restrictions. Teach the players the importance of testing and the benefits. Many tests can be affected by players' attitudes, so motivation and the timing of tests is important.

Tip 18 – Cross-training

This is a very important component, especially as the season comes to an end or when dealing with injury. Some of our best sessions, where players have both enjoyed themselves and worked extremely hard, have been in cross-training, e.g. swimming pool sessions, spinning classes, sessions on the beach, cycling outdoors, canoeing, etc. Not only do these sessions get the body working in different ways – improving overall fitness and resting muscles which are continually used with football-specific drills – but they also give players a change of scenery and keep them engaged and motivated.

Tip 19 – Use your imagination

Keep conditioning fresh, change locations, keep players guessing; do not be afraid to try variations and new ideas. Again, it is your responsibility to keep the players engaged in training.

Tip 20 – Keep it fun

At the right time and place, make conditioning fun and enjoyable if possible. For example, sprint work can be done in relays using batons, rugby or tennis balls, etc. For younger players especially, make conditioning as enjoyable as possible; you do not want children to lose their enthusiasm for playing soccer.

Tip 21 – Player competitiveness

Ninety per cent of players are highly competitive; use it to your advantage! Use teams in conditioning drills, keep a league table of players' results during the season, introduce a 'Fittest Player' award at the end-of-season celebrations. You can also include short and simple quizzes as part of this, focussing on nutrition and lifestyle factors, to educate players about issues that they are responsible for.

Tip 22 – Heart rate monitors

Although these are not infallible, as several lifestyle factors can affect readings, they are probably one of the best tools to monitor and test players. Once a player's maximum heart rate is known it is an invaluable piece of information as it can be used to determine the activity levels for that player (e.g. recovery heart rate, aerobic heart rate zone, anaerobic heart rate zone, etc.). Testing a player's resting heart rate and regularly monitoring this is also one of the best ways of checking whether a player is overtraining. Note that over a period of time a player's maximum heart rate will change, thus affecting the rates, so re-testing will be required.

Heart rate monitors are not suitable for younger players.

Tip 23 – Dynamic flexibility routines

Dynamic flexibility is one of my favourite stretching routines as it is close to what players do on the field of play. This includes exercises like knee swings, side leg swings, knee thrusts, wheeling, butt kicks, high-knee kicks, lunges, lateral lunges, goose-step and high-knee grab, etc. (For further information on these routines, see Pearson, A. *SAQ Soccer*, A&C Black.)

Tip 24 – Young players and children

This is another area that has its own chapter. Generally speaking, from growth spurt onwards (13/14–19-year-olds) young players should be introduced to many of the components of conditioning that the senior teams do. This is mainly to educate and prepare players of the future; some of the sessions may be adaptations of senior team sessions. For younger children (9–13/14) there is no harm in doing basic ladder work, turning techniques and running style.

Tip 25 – Hard work

Last, but certainly not least, there is no substitute for hard physical work, at the right time and place. All the sports science, nutritional information and gadgets will never replace the passion, desire and will to win.

APPENDIX 1:

Summary overview of six-week pre-season programme

Week 1						
M	T	W	T	F	S	S
Stadium/ Park	Stadium/ Park	RAF location	RAF location	Training		
10.00am Park: Runs + Strength Work	10.00am Gym: Runs + Strength Work	9.30am Interval Training + Strength Work + Pool	9.30am Interval Training + Strength Work + Pool	9.30am Testing; Strength Work + Head Tennis	OFF	OFF
4.00pm Training Ground Soccer	4.00pm Training Ground Soccer	pm off	4.00pm Soccer	pm off		
LOW	LOW/ MOD	MOD	MOD/ HIGH	MOD		

Week 2						
M	T	W	T	F	S	S
School location	School location	School location	School location	Training Ground		
am off	10.00am: Interval Training + Strength Work + Pool	10.00am: Interval Training + Strength Work + Pool	10.00am: Non-Running Day: Strength Work + Pool	10.30am Testing + Soccer	GAME 45 mins each player	OFF
1.00pm Interval Training + Strength Training	4.00pm: Soccer	4.00pm: Soccer	pm off	pm off		
MOD/ HIGH	HIGH	HIGH	MOD	LOW		

Week 3						
M	T	W	T	F	S	S
TOUR	TOUR	TOUR	TOUR	TOUR		
10.00am TRAVEL	Soccer + GAME	Recovery Day – am: Pool	10.00am: Speed Work + Soccer	Soccer + GAME	OFF	OFF
4.00pm: Speed Endurance + Soccer		pm off	pm off			
MOD		–	MOD			

Week 4						
M	T	W	T	F	S	S
Training Ground	Training Ground		Training	Training Ground		
10.00am: Soccer	Mainly Subs + Reserves – GAME; Rest of Squad – Training	OFF	10:00am: Testing + Strength Work	Soccer	GAME	OFF
4.00pm: Strength Work + Endurance Training			4.00pm: Soccer			
HIGH	GAME/ HIGH		MOD/ HIGH	LOW		

Week 5						
M	T	W	T	F	S	S
Training			Training Ground	Training Ground		
Soccer	GAME + Reserve Game	OFF	10.00am: Soccer + Speed Endurance	Soccer	GAME	OFF
			4.00pm: Soccer			
LOW/ MOD			HIGH	LOW		

Week 6						
M	T	W	T	F	S	S
Training Ground	Training Ground		Training Ground	Training		
10.00am: Soccer + Reserve Game; Testing + Strength Work	Soccer + Speed Endurance	OFF	Soccer	Soccer	START OF SEASON	
4.00pm: Soccer						
HIGH	HIGH		LOW	LOW		

APPENDIX 2:

Detailed plan of first week of pre-season Training

			Week 1	
Monday	10.00am	Stadium/ Park	6mins jog/stretches	Low intensity
			12mins jog; dynamic stretches	
			3 groups (rotate after 5 mins and 10 mins): Group 1: basic agility work Group 2: basic multi-direction work Group 3: basic speed work	
			Stretches; 6mins jog	
			40mins basic core stability, wobble board work, all-round strength work (dyno bands, medicine ball etc., 4 x physios)	
	4.00pm	Training ground	45mins basic soccer work with coaches	Low intensity
Tuesday	10.00am	Stadium health club	10mins jog; stretches	Low/ Moderate Intensity
			2 groups (rotate after 40mins): Group 1: 12mins run at 12.5kph; rest and stretch 3–4 mins; 12mins run at 14–16kph (depending on individual); rest and stretch.	
			Group 2: (In dance studio) Core stability, wobble board work, all-round strength work (dyno bands, medicine ball etc., 4 x physios)	Low intensity
	4.00pm	Training ground	45mins basic soccer work with coaches	

Wednesday	9.00am		Travel to RAF location	
	9.30am	RAF facilities	10mins jog; multi-directional warm-up; stretches	Moderate/High Intensity
			Basic speed drills/stretch (6mins max.)	
			2 groups (rotate after 32mins): Group 1: Fitness with a ball Group 2: Core stability, wobble board work, all-round strength, injury prevention work (physios)	
	11.20am		Pool session – 20mins fitness: 5 groups, based on swimming ability	
	pm	-	OFF	
Thursday	9.00am		Travel to RAF location	
	9.30am	RAF Facilities	10mins jog; multi-directional warm-up; stretches	Moderate Intensity
			Basic speed drills/stretch (6mins max.)	
			2 groups (rotate after 32mins): Group 1: Fitness with a ball Group 2: Core stability, wobble board work, all-round strength, injury prevention work (physios)	
	4.00pm	Training ground	1 hour soccer work with coaches	High Intensity
Friday	10.00am	Training ground	30mins warm-up/basic drills	High Intensity
			12mins run test	
			Mixed circuit training – emphasis on weights; core stability and head tennis	
	pm	–	OFF	
Saturday	–		OFF *Note – overweight players training	
Sunday	–		OFF	

INDEX